REFLECTING

REFLECTING

Complete Assemblies for Secondary Schools

JAN THOMPSON

Hodder & Stoughton

A MEMBER OF THE HODDER HEADLINE GROUP

For Juliet Sarah
'May she shine as a light in the world'

British Library Cataloguing in Publication Data

Thompson, Jan
Reflecting: Complete assemblies for
Secondary Schools.
1. Great Britain, Secondary Schools.
Morning assembly, Themes – For Schools
T. Title
377'.1

ISBN 0 340 42954 2

First published 1988
Impression number 14 13 12 11 10 9 8 7 6 5
Year 1998 1997 1996 1995 1994 1993

Printed in Great Britain for Hodder & Stoughton Educational, a division of Hodder Headline Plc, Mill Road, Dunton Green, Sevenoaks, Kent TN13 2YA by Athenaeum Press Ltd, Newcastle upon Tyne.

Acknowledgements

The publishers would like to thank the following for their kind permission to reproduce copyright material:

'One more step along the world I go' and 'There is a light that is shining', songs by Sydney Carter both reproduced by permission of Stainer & Bell Ltd., 'The Bear and the Travellers' from *Aesop's Fables*, reproduced by permission of Heinemann Ltd; the Scripture quotations contained herein are from the Revised Standard Version Bible, copyright 1946, 1952 and 1971 by the Division of Christian Education of the National Council of the Churches of Christ in the USA and are used by permission; 'Grape Expectation' extract from *The Sunday Times Magazine* (10.8.86) by Hugh Johnson, reproduced by permission of The Sunday Times; extract from *The Prophet* by Kahlil Gibran, by permission of Heinemann Ltd; extract from *New Internationalist* no. 155 by Harini Raghuveer, reproduced by permission of New International Publications Ltd; extracts from the Good News Bible copyright American Bible Society 1976, published by The Bible Societies and Collins (Matthew 7:1-5; 1 Corinthians 9:25-7; Psalm 51:10; Luke 18:10-14; 1 Timothy 6:17-18); 'Loneliness' by Barnaby Braithwaite, published by the Christian Education Movement and reproduced by permission; *Letters from the Desert* by Carlo Carretto, published and copyright 1972 by Darton, Longman and Todd Ltd, used by permission of the publishers; Genesis 3:1-7; John 13:3-5, 12-15 and 24; Luke 6:28-31; and Revelation 12:7-9, from the New English Bible, second edition, copyright 1970, reproduced by permission of Oxford and Cambridge University presses; extract from *Prose Poems* by Kahlil Gibran, by permission of Heinemann Ltd; extracts from *Paris Talks* by Abdul Baha, reproduced by permission of the Bahi'i Faith; *Rainbows of the Gutter* by Rukshana Smith, extracts reproduced by permission of The Bodley Head; extract from USPG'S *Network* magazine, April 1987, by Maggie and Anthony Barker, by permission of the United Society for the Propagation of the Gospel; extract from the speech by Martin Luther King from *The Pacifist*, January 1984, by permission of the Peace Pledge Union; extract from *Brave New World* by Aldous Huxley, by permission of Mrs Laura Huxley and Chatto & Windus, 'Musee de Beaux Arts' by W H Auden, by permission of Faber & Faber Ltd; extract from *Robin of Sherwood: The Hooded Man* by Anthony Horowitz, copyright Richard Carpenter and Anthony Horowitz by permission of Puffin Books; extract from *Mysteries and Problems* by Eric Lord, by permission of Longman; extract from John Betjeman's 'Harvest Hymn' taken from *Collected Poems*, by permission of the Lutterworth Press; Psalm 26: 1-4, 13-14 from *The Psalms: A New Translation for Worship* copyright English text 1976 and 1977 David L Frost, John A Emerson and Andrew A Macintosh, copyright for printing 1976 and 1977 William Collins & Sons Co. Ltd; 'I was Hungry' taken from *Assembly Workshop* by Roland Dingwall, published and copyright 1972 by Darton, Longman and Todd; extracts from *The Voyage of the Dawntreader* by C S Lewis, reproduced by permission of Collins; extract from an essay by Gillian Temple; extract from an essay by Kathryn Ungless; and a poem by Kathryn Ungless.

Every effort has been made to trace copyright holders of material reproduced in this book. Any rights not acknowledged here will be acknowledged in subsequent printings if notice is given to the publisher.

Contents

Peace

Suffering

Good and evil

Beliefs

Nature

Light

Assemblies suitable for special occasions

Occasion	Date	Assemblies	Page
New School Year		**Life's journey:** Setting out	2
		School	26
		Time: A time and a place for everything	11
Harvest		**Nature:** Thanksgiving	120
		Conservation	122
Michaelmas	29 September	**Good and evil:** St Michael	104
United Nations Day	24 October	**One World:** United Nations	80
Halloween	31 October	**Beliefs:** Superstition	115
Remembrance Sunday		**Peace:** Remembrance	92
Advent		**Light**	124
Christmas		**Light**	124
		Charity: Giving	70
		Beliefs: Images of God	110
New Year	1 January	**Life's journey:** No turning back	6
St Valentine's Day	14 February	**Love**	64
Half-term		**Time:** Half-term	16
Mothering Sunday		**Age:** Babies	18
		Children	20
		Teenagers	21
Spring		**Forgiveness:** A fresh start	60
Lent		**Forgiveness:** Guilt	58
		A fresh start	60
St George's Day	23 April	**Good and evil:** St George	102
Whitsun		**Beliefs:** An easy option?	112
School Examinations		**Tests:** If a thing's worth doing	33
		Keep calm	36
Sports Day		**Tests:** In training	34
End of Term		**Time:** Ends and beginnings	13
	Friday 13	**Beliefs:** Superstition	115

Preface

Reflecting is a collection of assemblies, used originally at a secondary school of mixed ages and abilities, where most pupils were not active members of any religion.

In presenting human feelings, beliefs and values, these assemblies encourage a reflective approach to life. They confront the ultimate questions which all human beings ask at some time or other, whether or not they would call themselves 'religious'. They try to raise issues rather than to give dogmatic answers.

The assemblies are made more explicitly religious in that each ends with a prayer, often of a meditative nature. This gives the listeners the opportunity to make the thoughts of the assembly their own, and to offer them up beyond themselves if they wish. These prayers can be used in a multi-faith situation.

The assemblies are written to be read out loud. Each is clearly printed on a new page for easy reference and is divided into sections of manageable length. Wherever possible, the wording has been kept simple and tongue-twisters have been avoided. This makes it suitable for the assemblies to be presented by pupils as well as teachers.

They are written to be listened to. They are not too long; and each assembly concentrates on just one main point. If presented by a number of readers, the change of voice with each section will make the assemblies sound more interesting.

The preparation of school assemblies is both a tremendous privilege and a responsibility, and is therefore very time consuming. It is my hope that those who organise them will appreciate these ready-made assemblies. Although complete in themselves, they can, of course, be enhanced with music; and a number on the same theme could be combined to form a longer service. For a more traditional Christian assembly, hymns, the Lord's Prayer and Bible readings could be added.

LIFE'S JOURNEY

Setting out

Life is often thought of as a journey, and all of us as travellers on life's road. We would be foolish to set out on any journey without knowing where we are going, without being properly prepared and without knowing the way. And for a very important journey – especially one we had never undertaken before – we should take advice from those who know most about the journey, consult maps and rely on trustworthy directions.

Growing up is a time of preparation for the great journey of life. School helps you to learn the skills you will need for that journey. It teaches you, trains you and tests you, so that you are prepared for anything you may encounter on your way.

School also helps you to think about the direction you want to go in, and the destination you want to arrive at. There are many roads open to us – many different ideas about the purpose of human life. Religions and religious leaders have claimed to be 'the way' or 'the path' or 'the door'; and they offer people a guide and a helper to go with them on life's journey. You will have the chance to consider some of these claims as you prepare for your own journey, and to test how true they are. It is hoped that, eventually, you will feel ready to set out on your own journey, knowing where you are going and how best to get there.

For our prayer today, we are going to think about some words from a Christian song. The writer, Sydney Carter, is addressing God.

Let us pray

One more step along the world I go,
One more step along the world I go,
From the old things to the new

Keep me travelling along with you.
And it's from the old I travel to the new,
Keep me travelling along with you.

Round the corners of the world I turn,
More and more about the world I learn.
And the new things that I see
You'll be looking at along with me.
And it's from the old I travel to the new,
Keep me travelling along with you.

As I travel through the bad and good
Keep me travelling the way I should.
Where I see no way to go
You'll be telling me the way, I know.
And it's from the old I travel to the new,
Keep me travelling along with you.

Give me courage when the world is rough,
Keep me loving though the world is tough.
Leap and sing in all I do,
Keep me travelling along with you.
And it's from the old I travel to the new,
Keep me travelling along with you.

You are older than the world can be,
You are younger than the life in me.
Ever old and ever new,
Keep me travelling along with you.
And it's from the old I travel to the new,
Keep me travelling along with you.

Amen

Change of direction

Conversion is a religious word, used when people become committed to a particular religious viewpoint. But all the word really means is to turn about, or change direction. Some people suddenly and dramatically change direction in the journey of life, starting out on something totally new to them. St Paul's conversion was like this. It changed his whole way of life – and it *literally* happened on a journey.

Paul was not one of Jesus' twelve disciples but, soon after Jesus' death, he became one of his greatest followers. It was Paul who took Christianity from Palestine to many other parts of the Mediterranean World. Yet this only came about after a remarkable conversion. Before that time, he was a Jewish scholar, determined to destroy Christianity. In fact, he had set out for Damascus, with permission to arrest any Christians he could find there. In a speech in the Book of Acts, Paul tells us what changed his mind:

> At midday . . . I saw on the way a light from heaven, brighter than the sun, shining round me and those who journeyed with me. And when we had all fallen to the ground, I heard a voice saying to me in the Hebrew language, 'Saul, Saul, why do you persecute me? . . . And I said, 'Who are you, Lord?' And the Lord said, 'I am Jesus whom you are persecuting. But rise and stand upon your feet; for I have appeared to you for this purpose, to appoint you to serve and bear witness to [me] to whom I send you, to open their eyes, that they may turn from darkness to light and from the power of Satan to God, that they may receive forgiveness of sins and a place among those who are sanctified by faith in me.'*

Saul changed his name to Paul; and this enemy of Christ became his devoted servant, working as energetically *for* him, as he had previously done against him.

Few people have such a dramatic experience as this – yet people do sometimes, like Paul, decide to change direction in their lives. It is not an easy decision to make. It takes a lot of soul-searching and a lot of courage. It often means giving up a steady job, and perhaps also moving to a new area. But if people feel that they have at last

* Acts 26: 13–18.

discovered the real purpose in their lives, then they will think all the upheaval is worthwhile.

Let us pray

LORD, if we are going in the wrong direction, in any aspect of our lives, please stop us, put us on the right path, and renew our strength to start again.

Amen

No turning back

Some of you will know the C. S. Lewis books about Narnia. The most famous is called *The Lion, the Witch and the Wardrobe*. It tells how four children get into the magic land of Narnia, where they have many adventures. In one of the sequels, Lucy has bravely gone into a magician's room, to try to find a spell which will help the poor creatures called Duffers.

> *The* book, the Magic Book, was lying on a reading desk in the very middle of the room. She went up to the desk and laid her hand on the book; her fingers tingled when she touched it as if it were full of electricity. There was no title page; the spells began straight away, and at first there was nothing very important. There were cures for warts and toothache and cramp. The picture of the man with toothache was so lifelike that it would have set your own teeth aching if you looked at it too long. Lucy could hardly tear herself away, but when she turned over, the next page was just as interesting. 'But I must get on,' she told herself. And on she went for about thirty pages.
>
> On the next page she came to a spell 'for the refreshment of the spirit'. The pictures were fewer here but very beautiful. And what Lucy found herself reading was more like a story than a spell. It went on for three pages, and before she had read to the bottom of the page she had forgotten that she was reading at all. She was living in the story as if it were real. When she had got to the third page and come to the end, she said, 'That is the loveliest story I've ever read or ever shall read in my whole life. Oh, I wish I could have gone on reading it for ten years. At least I'll read it over again.'
>
> But here part of the magic of the Book came into play. You couldn't turn back. The right-hand pages, the ones ahead, could be turned; the left-hand pages could not.

The Magic Book that can only be turned forwards, but never back, is a bit like life itself. There is no turning back on the road of life, although we often wish that we could. Perhaps, like Lucy, we should like to have something all over again, like a birthday, or Christmas, or a holiday that has come to an end too soon. Perhaps we regret something in the past, and would like to have a second chance at it. Looking back, we may think, 'If only I'd worked harder, I might have passed those exams.' 'If only I'd visited my grandmother more often before she died.' 'If only . . . if only . . . if only . . . ' We cannot change the past, but we can learn from it. As we go forward on life's journey, we can try to do better.

Let us pray

LORD, as we look back, we give thanks for all the opportunities we have had for making progress, and for all the people who have helped us on our way. We confess that we have sometimes wasted our opportunities: that we have loitered when we could have gone forward; and that we have sometimes taken the wrong road. Help us to learn from our past mistakes, and to go forward with courage into the future.

Amen

Journey's end

However pleasant a journey may be, it is good to arrive at our destination. We rarely travel just for the sake of it, but because we want to get somewhere. Sometimes journeys can be very difficult or even dangerous, and then it is a relief when they are over and we have arrived safely.

Yet the journey of life is very different! Most of us want to prolong it, and we would rather not reach our destination at all. Perhaps that's because we are unsure where we are going and what there is, if anything, at the end of the road.

Death is the one certain thing in life. Sooner or later, each one of us will reach our journey's end. Perhaps, after all, it will be a joy and relief to have arrived there. Perhaps the journey of life will all be worthwhile. Perhaps it will be the beginning of an even greater journey.

Psalm 23 – a very famous psalm from the Bible – is our prayer today. It is often read at funerals because it assures people that they can trust God to lead them through life, and through 'the valley of the shadow of death', to the best destination of all – to be with God for ever.

Let us pray

The LORD is my shepherd, I shall not want;
he makes me lie down in green pastures.
He leads me beside still waters;
he restores my soul.
He leads me in paths of righteousness
for his name's sake

Even though I walk through the valley of the shadow of death,
I fear no evil;
for thou art with me;
thy rod and thy staff,
they comfort me.

Thou preparest a table before me
in the presence of my enemies;
thou anointest my head with oil,
my cup overflows.
Surely goodness and mercy shall follow me
all the days of my life;
and I shall dwell in the house of the LORD for ever.*

Amen

* *Psalm 23.*

Travelling companions

'The Bear and the Travellers' from *Aesop's Fables*:

> Two Travellers were on the road together, when a Bear suddenly appeared on the scene. Before he observed them, one made for a tree at the side of the road, and climbed up into the branches and hid there. The other was not so nimble as his companion; and, as he could not escape, he threw himself on the ground and pretended to be dead. The Bear came up and sniffed all round him, but he kept perfectly still and held his breath: for they say that a bear will not touch a dead body. The Bear took him for a corpse, and went away.
>
> When the coast was clear, the Traveller in the tree came down, and asked the other what it was the Bear had whispered to him when he put his mouth to his ear. The other replied, 'He told me never again to travel with a friend who deserts you at the first sign of danger.'

Let us pray

There's a proverb which says, 'A friend in need is a friend indeed.' It is in times of need, when the going gets rough, that we realise who our true friends are. They don't desert us when we most need their help. They are people on whom we can rely.

We need friends to travel with us on life's journey. Sometimes we have things to give our friends: we can lend them a hand with what they're doing, or a friendly ear when they want to talk. At other times, *we* are the ones who need companionship and support. Friendship is sharing and caring; laughing and crying together; spending time with each other; learning from each other and with each other.

Help us, LORD, to value friendship, and never to let our friends down. Help us to be friends indeed.

Amen

TIME

A time and a place for everything

What does life consist of, if not time? Our lives are measured in months and years. The cynic might describe life simply as a waste of time – counting off the years from birth till death. But then, what would be the point of life?

Many people feel that life must have a purpose, and that time is our most precious gift. Without time we could not grow and develop as people; we could not form relationships; we could not make something with our lives. Time is described as the great healer, easing the pain of loss and grief. Time gives us the opportunity to make up for things, and to try again.

There is a famous poem in the Old Testament which speaks of the order of life, in which there is a time and a place for everything:

For everything there is a season,
and a time for every matter under heaven:
a time to be born, and a time to die;
a time to plant, and a time to pluck up what is planted;
a time to kill, and a time to heal;
a time to break down, and a time to build up;
a time to weep, and a time to laugh;
a time to mourn, and a time to dance;
a time to cast away stones, and a time to gather stones together;
a time to embrace, and a time to refrain from embracing;
a time to seek, and a time to lose;
a time to keep, and a time to cast away;
a time to rend, and a time to sew;
a time to keep silence, and a time to speak;
a time to love, and a time to hate;
a time for war, and a time for peace.*

* *Ecclesiastes 3:1–8.*

Let us pray

LORD, we thank you for the precious gift of time.
It's so easy to waste it:
to let the sands of time just trickle through our fingers.
Give us the wisdom to know when something is the right time,
and help us to use it to the full.

Amen

Ends and beginnings

Clement of Alexandria, a second-century Christian writer, said: 'The Lord has turned all our sunsets into sunrises.' He knew that every end is also a new beginning.

In nature, the plant dies, but its bulb or its seed puts forth new shoots again the following year. Human death also can be seen as a new beginning – whether from the religious point of view, that life in God goes on somehow – or from the humanist point of view, that we go on in our children and in all the ways we have influenced the world we leave behind.

But each human life is also a series of ends and beginnings: of deaths and resurrections. Birth is the end of the safe, secure life in the womb, when the baby is thrust out into the big, wide world. Yet we call this the beginning of a person's life.

How many deaths does a child die when his mother leaves him at play-school or infant school? But a whole new world of other people and new experiences is opening up to him.

When children reach the age of eleven, they leave behind their old school, where they belonged for seven years. But after the goodbyes comes the possibility of making new friends and learning from all the new opportunities of secondary school.

When young people leave school for good, there is a new beginning opening up for them, as they set out on the adventure and responsibility of adult life.

Even when people retire from work, they can look forward to having time for new experiences.

Each of these ends is a death in its own way – but, however painful, it is also a new beginning, a resurrection to new life.

Let us pray

LORD, we ask that you will turn all our sunsets into sunrises; that we will be able to bear the pain of parting from old friends and places, because of the new things we have to look forward to; that we will have the courage to accept all our 'deaths' as a means to new life.

Amen

Live for today

Old people often live in the past. They love to tell you, over and over again, of incidents which stand out in their memories. Sadly, they may reach a stage when the past is more real to them than the present; and they find their happiness in the past rather than in the future.

There are other people who seem to be always living for the future. They are always making plans about what they would like to do – but they never actually get round to doing it!

We cannot live our lives either in the past or in the future. The past might have many happy memories for us, but if we are always dwelling on them, we won't be able to appreciate the present. Neither should we let the past haunt us with regrets about what might have been, and about things which it is now too late to change.

Nor can we always be living for tomorrow, for we all know that 'tomorrow never comes'. We can have all the good intentions in the world – but the important thing is to start putting them into practice, here and now. It is *today* that counts, as this very ancient Indian poem points out:

Look to this day!
For it is life, the very life of life.
In its busy course
Lie all the virtues and realities of your existence:
The bliss of growth,
The glory of action,
The splendour of achievement.
For yesterday is but a dream,
Tomorrow is only a vision,
But today well lived makes yesterday a dream of happiness
And every tomorrow a vision of hope.
Look well therefore to this day.

Let us pray

LORD, help us to enjoy the present moment –
to value this day for its own sake,
for today will never be repeated.

Amen

Half-term

It's 7 a.m.
Time to get up for school
But not today!
Turn over and go back to sleep
And tomorrow
And for the whole of the week.

8 o'clock now?
Time I had left for school
No, not today!
I'm warm and I need the sleep
And tomorrow
And for the rest of the week.

Stay in bed
Time to relax and unwind
Time to read
Time to just think and to be
Plenty of time
this week, to drift and to dream.

Time to get up
when I feel I'm up to it
Time to catch up
on the things I've been wanting to do
Time to tidy up
Time to dress up and go somewhere new.

A whole week of time
Time to look in the shops
Time to breathe
Time to drink coffee and chat
And no one
breathing down my neck.

It's 10 p.m.
Better be getting to bed
School tomorrow
Doesn't half-term go fast?
All that time
A pity it doesn't last!

Let us pray

Thank you, LORD, for holiday-time.
For time to do what we like.
Help us to make the most of it,
And to think of others as well as ourselves.
May we return afterwards
Refreshed and renewed.

Amen

AGE

Babies

A new-born baby, so small and helpless, is nevertheless a positive sign of hope. Having babies is a way of saying 'Yes' to life.

The long months of waiting, and the painful hours of labour, are forgotten at the moment of birth. Thoughts of sleepless nights ahead are pushed aside by the joy of seeing the baby at last. The fears and doubts and worries of parenthood are swamped by feelings of relief and pride. Parents share together their secret hopes for their children; and resolve how they intend to bring them up. Cards arrive, congratulating the happy couple, and wishing the child all that is best in life.

At times like this, life seems to have purpose, it seems to be worthwhile. We look to the future, determined to overcome the problems which threaten to diminish or even destroy human existence on this planet.

The theme of New Life/New Hope is expressed by two 'wise men' of this century. Rabindranath Tagore, the Indian playwright and poet, said:

> Every child that comes into the world
> brings the message that God has not yet despaired of man.

And the Western psychiatrist, R. D. Laing, said:

> Each time a new baby is born there is a possibility of reprieve. Each child is a new being, a potential prophet, a spiritual prince, a new spark of light precipitated into the outer darkness. Who are we to decide that it is hopeless?

Let us pray

It was a long time ago now,
but once we were all new-born babies,
bringing happiness to those who love us,
and filling them with hopes for our future.
LORD, help us to be inspired by their love and their hopes;
and may we continue to be a source of delight and pride.

Amen

Children

Hugh Johnson, a wine expert and journalist, writes about his eighteen-year-old daughter in this way:

> Lucy was our first child and I was there when she was born. From that moment I was captivated, fascinated by watching her grow up . . . The thing which I found quite overwhelming, as she grew, was the emerging sense that this person had nothing to do with me. I realised that one's children are absolute strangers for whom one is responsible. I think it is a central feature of our relationship because I have never felt it would be right to try to mould Lucy or dictate what she should do.

Of course our parents are ambitious for us. They may even try to mould us into the sort of people *they* want us to be – or even the sort of people they would like to have been themselves.

But really they have known all along, from the moment their children were born, that each one has its own personality. The best that parents can do for their children is to give them the security and the freedom to allow them to develop as individuals.

The religious poet, Kahlil Gibran, puts it like this:

> You may give them your love but not your thoughts,
> For they have their own thoughts.
> You may house their bodies but not their souls,
> For their souls dwell in the house of tomorrow, which you cannot visit,
> not even in your dreams.
> You may strive to be like them, but seek not to make them like you.
> For life goes not backward nor tarries with yesterday.

Let us pray

LORD, we thank you for our parents who gave us birth,
who took on the responsibility of bringing us up,
and who have made many sacrifices for us.
Thank you also for giving us our own individual personalities,
and our own special paths to tread in life.

Amen

Teenagers

How often have you heard an adult say: '*I* was never allowed to do that when I was your age.' Or, 'Whatever are young people coming to these days?' What about the following statements?

> When I was a boy, we were taught to be discreet and respectful of elders, but the present youth are exceedingly impatient of restraint. They have detestable manners, flout authority, have no respect for their elders. What kind of creatures will they be when they grow up?

> The young people of today think of nothing but themselves. They have no reverence for parents or old age. They are impatient of all restraint. They talk as if they alone know everything.

The funny thing is, that both of these were written hundreds of years ago. The first is by the Greek poet Hesiod, from the eighth century BC; and the other by Peter the Monk who lived in the thirteenth century AD.

So it seems that young people haven't changed all that much down through the ages. And adults were the same as us in *their* youth – perhaps it's just too long ago for them to remember!

Teenagers have always needed to spread their wings, to try out new experiences and have a bit of fun. That's how we discover who we are – what we're really like – before we get sobered up by the heavy responsibilities of paying the mortgage and bringing up our own children.

Let us pray

LORD, in our enthusiasm, help us not to be so thoughtless that we harm either ourselves or others. Help us to come to understand ourselves better, and to be more ready to take on the responsibilities of adult life.

Amen

Adults

I remember, I remember
The fir-trees dark and high;
I used to think their slender tops
Were close against the sky.
It was a childish ignorance,
But now 'tis little joy
To know I'm farther off from heaven
Than when I was a boy.

Children always want to be a year older; and teenagers look forward to the time when they can lead their own lives, without their parents and teachers breathing down their necks. But growing up can be a painful and difficult process. It is when we become more aware of ourselves and of others. It means admitting that we are not perfect, and coming to terms with the sides of our nature we would rather pretend did not exist. It means recognising that the adults in our lives are fallible too – even those we admire and on whom we rely. It means facing up to the dark side of life: the cruelty with which people treat each other; the greed and injustice in the world.

Everything which seemed so straightforward to us as children now becomes more complicated. There are at least two sides to every argument. We change our minds about things we once held certain. Doubts creep in where once we had faith. Growing up can be a disturbing time. Heaven seems so much farther off now. But we cannot stay children for ever. We must learn to face up to our human condition. We must find the best way of making the most of it – the best way, not just for ourselves, but for all whose lives we touch in any way.

Let us pray

We'll finish with Thomas Hood's poem once more. It has a ring of pessimism about it, and nostalgia for the innocence of childhood. But, for all the pain, growing to maturity can be a challenge to discover a more real idea of heaven.

I remember, I remember
The fir-trees dark and high;
I used to think their slender tops
Were close against the sky.
It was a childish ignorance,
But now 'tis little joy
To know I'm farther off from heaven
Than when I was a boy.

Amen

Old people

What will it be like to grow old? To gradually lose our independence? To be at the mercy of others?

Mrs Gates was a dear old lady.
She would toddle out of her house whenever she saw us in the back garden.
She would accept ice-creams from us – childlike – over the fence;
and in return, she would press us to take apples,
and biscuits for the dog.
She would ask us the same questions and tell us the same stories
over and over again.
We loved her – with her woolly hat, and squint eyes.
There was no harm in her.

Then one day, three young men forced their way into her house,
and stole her savings.
They pretended to be workmen, checking the gas.
They did her no physical harm,
but after that she was afraid to be alone
in the house where she had come as a bride, fifty years before.
She would imagine there were people hiding in the wardrobe
or under the bed.
She would tremble like a leaf;
and when I put my arm round her, she felt frail as a bird.

There was no room in the old people's home,
so they put her in hospital – in a psychiatric ward.
She didn't survive long there.

A young Hindu journalist, living in London, says:

It seems that there's very little respect for the sanctity of life in our so-called civilised world. But we have to start somewhere. So in my life I try and give as much time as I can to help other people. I see it is my duty to help others.

I have an English neighbour, an elderly widow who is almost blind. I pop in every day to read her the papers. I suppose eventually she'll end up in an old people's home. That is unthinkable in Indian society.

Our religion teaches us to respect the elderly – not for what they say or do, but because they are our elders.

Let us pray

Help us, LORD, to have respect for the elderly, to sympathise with their needs, and to do all we can to help them.

Amen

SCHOOL

Community

A community is a body of people who share something in common. School is a community – where we live together for a large part of the week, and where we work together for the common purpose of education.

In this reading from the New Testament, St Paul reminds his readers in Corinth, that *everyone* in a community is important, and should therefore be treated with respect; and that we depend upon each other to do our work well. He uses the imagery of a physical body to put across these points:

> The body does not consist of one member but of many. If the foot should say, 'Because I am not a hand, I do not belong to the body,' that would not make it any less a part of the body. And if the ear should say, 'Because I am not an eye, I do not belong to the body,' that would not make it any less a part of the body. If the whole body were an eye, where would be the hearing? If the whole body were an ear, where would be the sense of smell? But as it is, God arranged the organs in the body, each one of them, as he chose. If all were a single organ, where would the body be? As it is, there are many parts, yet one body. The eye cannot say to the hand, 'I have no need of you,' nor again the head to the feet, 'I have no need of you.' . . .
>
> God has so composed the body . . . that there may be no discord in the body, but that the members may have the same care for one another. If one member suffers, all suffer together; if one member is honoured, all rejoice together.*

Let us pray

LORD, you have gathered us together into one body
so that we now belong to each other.

* *1 Corinthians 12:14–26.*

Help us to respect every member of this community,
for we each have our part to play.
Help us to get on with each other,
and to work smoothly together,
for the common good.

Amen

Tolerance

What qualities do you think are necessary to get on with other people? Surely one of the most important is tolerance.

Tolerance comes from recognising and accepting that we are all *different*, and that life would be pretty dull if everyone was the same. We sometimes act as though we expect everyone to be just like us.

It comes from trying to *understand* why people are like they are, instead of just reacting to what they do.

It comes from respecting other people's right to *their* point of view, even if we don't agree with them.

And it comes from accepting the fact that *we* are not perfect. Only when we come to terms with our own limitations will we be less critical of other people's failings, because we won't expect them to be perfect either.

Jesus made this last point in his typically exaggerated way and pictorial style:

> 'Do not judge others, so that God will not judge you, for God will judge you in the same way as you judge others, and he will apply to you the same rules you apply to others. Why, then, do you look at the speck in your brother's eye, and pay no attention to the *log* in your own eye? How dare you say to your brother, 'Please let me take that speck out of your eye,' when you have a log in your own eye? You hypocrite! First take the log out of your own eye, and then you will be able to see clearly to take the speck out of your brother's eye.'*

Let us pray

We give thanks for the rich variety of personalities here in school.
May we live together in harmony, respecting one another,
learning to give and take,
and growing in understanding and tolerance
both of others and of ourselves.

Amen

* *Matthew 7:1–5.*

Growth

W. H. Auden, a famous English poet of our day, said this:

> People cannot grow unless they are happy and, even when their material needs have been satisfied, they still need many other things. They want to be liked and to like other people; to feel valuable, both in their own eyes and in the eyes of others; to feel free and to feel responsible; above all, not to feel lonely and isolated.

School should be a place where we can grow. Not just physically – some of us don't want to get any larger! – but also in mind and spirit. We hope that we can create the sort of environment in which we *can* grow.

W. H. Auden said *we need to be liked – and to like one another*. The two things usually go together: if we're friendly to other people, they will usually be friendly to us.

He said *we need to feel valuable and valued*. None of us is good at everything, but we are all good at something. We all have something to offer. We must learn to look for what is best in ourselves and in others.

He said *we must feel free and responsible*. We need to be trusted with things, and to prove that we are trustworthy. We need to be free to take our own decisions and to do things for ourselves. Only then will we grow in self-confidence and become morally mature.

Auden said that, above all, *we mustn't feel lonely and isolated*. School is a community where we can work together. Everyone has his or her part to play. No one should feel lonely if we are a caring community.

Let us pray

LORD, help us to care for each other, to encourage our friends and colleagues, to respect those in authority over us, and to be considerate to those who keep the buildings clean for us. Help us to notice anyone who needs a smile and a friendly word, that we may build together a caring community in which each one of us may grow.

Amen

Loneliness

Loneliness is the old man who lives – and dies – alone in his flat. Nobody calls from one day to the next, because nobody really cares.

But loneliness can also be felt among crowds of people, when everyone else seems to be chatting happily, and one person is left out: 'Loneliness is an island – in the middle of a sea of people.'

The following verses are by a twelve-year-old boy on starting a new school. He expresses feelings which any of us might have at a new school, or a new job, or when doing anything for the first time, when we're joining other people who already know each other:

You try to join in
But they don't care
They just leave you alone
Standing there.
You try again to tell them
But you won't get through
They don't bother with some people
Especially not you!

You feel down and alone
With bad thoughts in your head
You wish you were at home
Just lying there in bed.

Other first formers have said:
'I had hardly any friends, and wondered how I was going to make new ones.'
'I was worried about meeting other people and other teachers.'
'I remember feeling smart – and trembly!'

One way to get friends is to make the effort ourselves. We could go out of our way to be friendly to others, instead of just waiting for them to make the first move. There is a lot of truth in the saying: 'Be a friend – the rest will follow.' But we could also be particularly sensitive to those who seem to be left out, and do all we can to include them, and make them feel welcome.

Let us pray

We all know what it's like to feel lonely.
We may be feeling particularly lonely at the moment;
there are certainly other people in school who are.
Let us think what it is like to be lonely:
'Loneliness is an island
in the middle of a sea of people.'

* * *

It's natural to be nervous in a new situation;
none of us is too old or too important to feel trembly inside;
many of us are shy about meeting new people.
Let us be helpful and sympathetic to new pupils and members of staff, and go out of our way to make them feel at home.

Amen

TESTS

Tried and tested

What are tests for? Tests are applied in all walks of life. Products are tested before being put on the market, and their weak points are improved. Doctors run tests on their patients, to find out what is wrong with them, in order to treat them.

At school, tests are a way of assessing our standard, so that we are given the right level of work. They may be used to check whether we have done the reading or learning that was set. They keep us up to scratch, making sure that we do not forget things. They are supposed to find out what we know and what we can do; but they often seem to show up what we don't know and what we can't do. So tests demonstrate both our strengths and our weaknesses.

It is not just our intelligence and our skills which can be tested, but also the strength of our characters. It is only when we are put to the test that we are able to prove ourselves. It is only when we withstand temptations that we know how strong we are.

Two areas in which this is clearly shown are in friendship and in religious faith. There may be times when we are tempted to desert our friends; when it would be easier to pretend we did not know them. But standing by our friends at such times seals our friendship.

Similarly, there are times when a person's faith is severely tested. In times of suffering, for instance, it is difficult to continue to believe in a God of love. But it is often through personal suffering that people gain strength from their religion; and having to wrestle with doubts, often deepens their faith in God.

Let us pray

LORD, we pray never to be tested beyond our powers of endurance. May tests demonstrate our good points, rather than our weaknesses, so that we come through them even stronger than before.

Amen

If a thing's worth doing

There is a saying, 'If a thing's worth doing, it's worth doing well.' We might think this is a good proverb at any time, but particularly when we take tests, when we certainly want to be successful. There is also some truth in a slightly altered version of that saying: 'If a thing's worth doing, it's worth doing badly!' In other words, it's worth trying hard, even if we are not one of those who always comes out on top. Indeed, there is often more to be learnt in life from failure than from success. One important lesson is how to be a good loser.

The New Testament records how Jesus turned things round to say what people least expected; and although these sayings may be difficult to understand, they certainly make you think. For instance, he said:

> 'Whoever would be great among you must be your servant.'
> 'If anyone would be first he must be last of all.'*

It seems that Jesus challenged the standards by which we normally assess people. So perhaps we should not judge ourselves too harshly if, having done our best, we do not pass tests with flying colours. It may be that those of us who fail tests will learn more than the rest about ourselves and about life. And if we are able to feel pleased for those who have done well, and don't give up trying but learn from our mistakes, then perhaps we shall come top in God's eyes.

Let us pray

LORD, grant to each of us the spirit of humility,
that we may always do our best
and try not to compare ourselves, favourably or unfavourably, with others.
You have shown us what is good, and told us what you require of us:
to do what is right, to be kind, and to walk humbly with you.

Amen

* *Matthew 20:26; Mark 9:35.*

In training

When we watch sports events, and the winners receiving their medals, we may wish that that could be us. But the excitement of the finals or the big match, and the glamour of the stars, may prevent us from realising how much hard training everyone has put into it. We see only the final test for which the competitors have been preparing for years. Their training can be very demanding and not always enjoyable in itself. Sportsmen and women must constantly watch their diet, exercise regularly and have early nights. Their training may mean getting up very early in the morning and then returning to it again after a normal day's work. It may be expensive, and leave little time for other things. Presumably it is all worthwhile – the enjoyment and sense of achievement – but it's a high price to pay and demands total commitment.

In the New Testament, St Paul uses the analogy of a sportsman to describe his religious life. He lived, not for sport, but for Christianity; but he argued that this demands the same dedication and that the prize at the end is far more worthwhile.

> Every athlete in training submits to strict discipline, in order to be crowned with a wreath that will not last; but we do it for one that will last for ever. That is why I run straight for the finishing line; that is why I am like a boxer who does not waste his punches. I harden my body with blows and bring it under complete control, to keep myself from being disqualified after having called others to the contest.*

Let us pray

Nothing is achieved without effort.
What do *we* think is really worthwhile in life?
Is there anything on which we would willingly spend our time – our energy – and our money?
What is worthy of our total commitment?

* *1 Corinthians 9:25–7.*

And if we find nothing for which we are prepared to give things up,
will we get any satisfaction out of life?
Or will we be left with regrets that we never entered the more
difficult contests?

Amen

Keep calm

There will be times in all of our lives when, for one reason or another, we come under stress. At examination time, for instance, many people are under pressure – not just those taking the exam, but those preparing them for it, and those marking the scripts, who have to get them finished by a particular date. At times like this, we need to find inner strength which will keep us from panicking and help us to make the best of the situation. Some of us panic when we are faced with revision: we do not know where to start and how we can get through it. Some of us panic much later, as we wait for the results-envelope to arrive in the post. Many of us panic in the examination itself, as in this somewhat unusual example where a teacher is doing an examination:

> 'It is now 9 a.m. precisely. You may turn over your examination paper and begin.'
>
> That sentence is familiar to many of you, but it's been ten years since I last sat an exam. As teachers, we invigilate them and mark them, but forget what an ordeal examinations are for those doing them. But now, here I am, sitting at my little desk, in a long row, in this large, cold room. I have an irresistible urge to giggle, but manage to control myself by concentrating on the graffiti on my desk. At '9 a.m. precisely' I obediently turn over the paper. I stare in horror as I read one question after another in sheer disbelief, convinced they've given me the wrong paper. I sit here stupefied as the clock slowly ticks away the minutes – my mind a complete blank, my stomach queasy, my hands sweating, my throat dry. I've got to pull myself together! At last I put pen to paper, and write as though my life depended on it.
>
> Afterwards, when the papers have been collected in and the silence is broken by everyone talking at once, I discover that we all found it difficult – and they can't fail us all – can they? I'm ashamed to say that I feel even better when Jane admits that she misread a word, so changing the whole meaning of one of the questions; and Know-All David realises that he didn't even see the last question on the back of the paper!
>
> Whatever the results, I don't want to do another examination as long as I live. And I promise to be more sympathetic to my own pupils in future!

How do we find inner strength to cope with times of stress, like this, so that we can keep calm, show ourselves at our best, and not make silly mistakes? There are some people who naturally rise to the occasion. They have a strength of character on which they can rely when they most need it. It is possible to train ourselves – through yoga or meditation, for instance – to be more calm and self-disciplined. And some people turn to God at such times, trusting that there is an infinite source of strength and peace available, if only they will allow the Spirit of God to work within them.

Let us pray

FATHER, we thank you for the love and support of our families and friends, when we are worried or overworked.
We thank you, also, for the inner strength which you offer us at such times through the power of your Spirit;
and that you can help us to meet the demands of each new day.

Amen

WORDS

Right speech

There is an old saying: 'Sticks and stones might break my bones, but words will never hurt me.' It is, in fact, not true. Broken bones can usually be mended, but thoughtless or spiteful words can make a much deeper impression on us.

Because words are so powerful, there is no lack of advice on how to use them, and many warnings. The New Testament tells Christians:

> No human being can tame the tongue – a restless evil, full of deadly poison. With it we bless the Lord and Father, and with it we curse men, who are made in the likeness of God. From the same mouth come blessing and cursing.*

One of the basic teachings of Buddhism is 'Right Speech' – encouraging Buddhists to use their words for good and not evil.

And here are some wise sayings on the subject from the religion of Islam:

> Beware of your tongue: it's like an arrow that often goes off course.
> Politeness costs nothing, but buys everything.
> The man who listens to gossip is bound to be a gossip himself.
> The person who tells you gossip is bound to gossip about you behind your back.
> Words are like medicine: a small dose can cure an illness; but too much can kill.
> As a person gets wiser, he speaks fewer words.

Let us pray

LORD, because we are sensitive ourselves,
help us to be sensitive about the feelings of others.

* *James 3:8–10.*

Guard our tongue from the angry word, spoken in haste
and immediately regretted;
From the thoughtless word which causes offence
without our intention;
From the insolent word, which shows no respect;
From spiteful comments and malicious gossip.
Help us to think before we speak;
To be polite and considerate;
And to use our words to encourage and help others,
rather than to harm them.

Amen

Telling lies

'Do you ever tell lies?'
'Are you always truthful?'
'Have you ever been dishonest with anyone?'
These are the sort of trick questions that you might come across in questionnaires. They are lie-detectors, put there to measure how truthfully you are answering the rest of the questions – because it is reckoned that all of us tell lies sometimes.

I expect we have all told fibs. You know the sort of thing. It's illustrated by this question from the game called Scruples: 'A friend has just bought an expensive painting and asks if you like it. You think it is awful. Do you say so?' Some people are tactful enough to get out of this situation without hurting anyone's feelings. Some are honest but far too blunt. Others resort to a fib.

But we may be able to remember telling a lie which was far worse than this. Perhaps it was to save face, or to get ourselves out of trouble – it may even have got someone else into trouble. This poem tells us 'Five Ways of Looking at a Lie' – that's its title:

A lie is like a nettle sting, you forget about it then it returns worse than ever.
A lie is like a window, you cover it up, but the curtains open to show people what you have done.
A lie is like a buzzing fly, it buzzes through your thoughts to torment you.
A lie is like a light switch, your conscience forces you to press it to light up your lie.
A lie is like a meandering river which keeps branching off to other directions, one lie leads to many lies.

Let us pray

LORD, help us to be truthful with ourselves, and in our dealings with others. We know that one lie leads to another, and it is better to own up and put the record straight. Please give us the courage to do that.

Amen

To speak or not to speak?

Most of us love talking. But do we ever stop to think why? There are, of course, very good uses for language. Where would we be without it? But some of us are real chatterboxes – we just cannot keep quiet.

Does this simply show a lack of self-discipline? Is it a good sign – because we are being sociable? Or are we, perhaps, afraid of silence? Afraid to be alone with our thoughts? Afraid of those 'embarrassing silences' when we are with people? Do we sometimes hide behind our words? This poem explores some of these ideas:

And then a scholar said, Speak of talking.
And he answered, saying:
You talk when you cease to be at peace with your thoughts;
And when you can no longer dwell in the solitude of your heart you live in your lips, and sound is a diversion and a pastime.
And in much of your talking, thinking is half murdered.
For thought is a bird of space, that in a cage of words may indeed unfold its wings but cannot fly.

There are those among you who seek the talkative through fear of being alone.
The silence of aloneness reveals to their eyes their naked selves and they would escape.
And there are those who talk, and without knowledge or forethought reveai a truth which they themselves do not understand.
And there are those who have the truth within them, but they tell it not in words.
In the bosom of such as these the spirit dwells in rhythmic silence.

Let us pray

Give us wisdom, LORD GOD, to know when to speak and when to keep silent. Let us not talk for its own sake, nor be afraid to speak when we must. Help us to be at peace with ourselves, so that we may feel confident both when we speak, and when we choose not to.

Amen

Silence

Mothers of small children often long for a few moments of 'peace and quiet'. Teachers are always asking their classes to stop talking. We love to chat; but sometimes 'silence is golden', and we need to be alone with our thoughts.

Silence and solitude are necessary if we want to have an inner life – a spiritual life. Many people feel the need sometimes to leave behind their busy working lives and homes, to go on retreat to a place of quiet. This passage was written by a monk in Algeria, where it is the practice for them to go into the Sahara Desert to be alone in prayer:

> The great joy of the Sahara is the solitude, and the silence, true silence, which penetrates everywhere and invades one's whole being, speaking to the soul with wonderful new strength unknown to men to whom this silence means nothing.

Then he begins to analyse this need for 'desert' in us all:

> When one speaks of the soul's desert, and says that the desert must be present in your life, you must not think only of the Sahara or the desert of Judea. Certainly it is not everyone who can have the advantage of being able to carry out in practice this detachment from daily life. But if you cannot go into the desert, you must nonetheless 'make some desert' in your life. Every now and then leaving people and looking for solitude to restore, in prolonged silence and prayer, the stuff of your soul. This is the meaning of 'desert' in your spiritual life. You must leave everything and everybody and retire, alone with God.

Let us pray

While we have this opportunity, let us rest for a few moments in the silence, and in the solitude of our inner thoughts . . .

> FATHER, we pray for your presence this day so that in all the rush and bustle of our comings and goings we may know your peace in our hearts.
>
> *Amen*

PRAYER

Keep at it

Suppose you have locked up for the night, switched off the lights and gone to bed. You have just dropped off to sleep when, at midnight, you are woken by a soft persistent tapping at the back door. You get out of bed and peer through the window to see who it is.

'Hello,' calls up a voice. 'It's only me. I haven't woken you up have I? I just wondered if you could let me have some food – anything will do – some friends have called on me unexpectedly and I've nothing to give them.' It's your next door neighbour, wanting to borrow something – as usual! Doesn't she know what time it is? You don't say what you're thinking, just, 'Sorry, I can't help you this time,' and slam the window shut.

You climb back into bed, still fuming, and try to get to sleep. But there's that knocking again – louder this time. Can't she take a hint? You bury your head under the duvet and try not to listen. You've got to get to sleep – it's Monday morning tomorrow and you've got to be up early for school. But she's still knocking – and calling out your name now. Next door's dog has started to bark. The whole street will be awake soon! This time, you jump out of bed, run downstairs and grab whatever food you can lay your hands on. 'Here. Take it,' you say. Anything for a bit of peace!

When Jesus told a story like this, he was teaching people about prayer. It was the persistence of the person at the door which eventually got her what she needed. In the same way, Jesus taught that we should not give up on prayer too easily. Prayer shouldn't be something we try out once or twice, and then give up when it doesn't seem to work. Prayer is meant to be an on-going communication between people and God. Sometimes people find that God is easy to reach, and their prayers are very fulfilling. At other times it might be more difficult. The important thing, for people who value prayer, is to keep at it.

Let us pray

LORD, when we find it difficult to pray, help us to keep on trying.
For you have assured us that:
When we ask, we shall receive – help us to keep asking for you;
When we seek, we shall find – help us to keep on seeking you;
And when we knock, the door will be opened – please open up the way to you.

Amen

Contemplatives

Many monks and nuns can be found doing good work out among the people: like nursing the sick, caring for the mentally ill and living among the poor. But there are others who stay within a monastery and devote their whole lives to prayer. They are known as contemplatives. This may seem to many of us to be a complete waste of a life. But perhaps they are there as a disturbing reminder that there is more to life than our busy concern with our own affairs.

Sheila Cassidy, a Christian doctor in Chile, discovered that time spent in quiet prayer was not such a waste of time after all:

> Unable to sleep after I had worked all night at the hospital, I used to take the little bus which went up into the hills and then walk up the steep dirt road to the monastery. The monks became used to me sitting in my poncho and jeans in the front row of their empty church . . . Thus we prayed together many times, the monks and I, high above Santiago.
>
> The presence of contemplatives in an active society is always disturbing. The folly of their life spent in prayer and manual labour is a curious sign of the existence of God in a world so preoccupied with its own affairs. I used to look at these men, the old ones who had wasted their life in this crazy way and the young ones who were freely choosing to do likewise, and wonder what on earth God wanted of me.
>
> It was a good place to come to pray and to think because, it being a long way, I had to be very desperate before I decided to go home. Sometimes they gave me lunch, and sometimes I took an apple and some cheese and sat on the low wall outside the church and overlooking the city stretched out below me . . . Then, stiff and sunburned, I would walk down the hill into the setting sun and know in some incommunicable way that my day had been well spent.

Let us pray

LORD, we thank you for those who remind us that the best use of our time is to spend it in prayer, concentrating on you. Not everyone can spend their whole life in prayer. Help the rest of us, whatever we are doing, to remember that we live in your presence always.

Amen

It's a help

A teenager remarked in amazement, 'I tried praying. And it worked!' She did not mean that she had bombarded God with a list of all the things she wanted, and found them waiting on the doorstep when she got home. She was sensible enough to realise that God was not just a sort of Father Christmas. What she meant was that time spent in prayer had been helpful to her. She had been upset and worried about something, and it had calmed her down; it had given her a chance to put things into perspective and to decide what to do next. It had worked because, through prayer, she had found peace of mind.

This girl had discovered that God listened to her and understood her. You might say that she could have talked things over with a friend. But, however close are our friends and family, and however much time they have to give us, other people can never really understand what it feels like to be me. In all important matters, however much advice people give us, in the end we are on our own. *We* have to decide how to live our lives. No one can really stand in our shoes. Yet people claim to find God deep within them: closer than their own heartbeat or their own breath. They find that God knows them better than they know themselves, and wants only what is best for them.

The following passage is called 'I've got to talk to somebody, God':

Let us pray

There are all these walls between us – husband and wife, parent and child, neighbour and neighbour, friend and friend.

Walls of self. Walls of silence. Even walls of words. For even when we try to talk to each other, new walls begin to rise. We camouflage, we hold back, we make ourselves sound better than we really are. Or we are shocked and hurt by what is revealed. Or we sit privately in judgement criticizing even when we pretend to agree. But with you, LORD, there are no walls.

You, who made me, know my deepest emotions, my most secret thoughts. You know the good of me and the bad of me; you already understand.

Why, then, do I turn to you?

Because as I talk to you my disappointments are eased, my joys are enhanced. I find solutions to my problems, or the strength to endure what I must.

From your perfect understanding I receive understanding for my own life's needs.

Thank you that I can always turn to you. I've got to talk to somebody, God.

Amen

Listening

We may assume that prayers have to have words. You can make up prayers and write them down. You can buy books of prayers. *But prayer is listening to God as well as speaking*. Of course, we cannot hear God in the same way as we hear other people. We cannot get a tape-recording of God's voice. Many people believe that God speaks to us through our inner promptings – when our conscience pricks us, or when special thoughts come to us. And people of all religions usually set aside special times when they can still their minds and shut out all the busy-ness of the day. Then they are ready to hear God's voice in their hearts. Hinduism, Judaism and the Baha'i Faith are religions which encourage their followers to pray three times a day. First thing in the morning and last thing at night are good times – when we can usually have a few moments to ourselves. And in hot countries, noon – in the heat of the day – is also a quiet time.

This poem is called 'In the Silence' and it expresses these ideas:

Seek me in the silence
For my voice
Is not in the earthquake
Wind or fire
But a still small voice
Speaking softly
To your heart
. . .
I speak
In the silence of the dawn
Before the busy world awakes;
In the noontide
When earth takes its rest;
In the evening
When the dusk falls softly;
During the night watch
To waking hearts.
But I will not shout
To make my voice heard
Amongst the clamour
Of earthly things

Of crowding thoughts.
You must listen
You must learn to love the silence
For it is then that I speak to you
In the quiet of your heart.

Let us pray

LORD, if only we would stop for a while, put aside our everyday concerns, and be still – you would meet us in the silence. If we listen, we will hear your still, small voice, speaking deep within us. We can find you in the silence . . .

Amen

HUMAN NATURE

In the image of God

> Then God said, 'Let us make man in our image, after our likeness; and let them have dominion over the fish of the sea, and over the birds of the air, and over the cattle, and over all the earth, and over every creeping thing that creeps upon the earth.' So God created man in his own image, in the image of God he created him; male and female he created them.*

In what sense are human beings made in the image of God?

It can't mean that we look like God, for God – by definition – is not a physical being. He cannot have a physical body like us, if he existed before the creation of the physical world.

So how do we resemble God?

Religious people would say that we are in the image of God because we too are creative. We all need a creative outlet, and find satisfaction in things like art, craft and technology, poetry and literature.

We have brains with which to reason things out; we can plan ahead, and change the environment in which we live.

We each have a conscience and the ability to tell right from wrong.

We can enjoy personal relationships, and can experience love.

Each of us, therefore, has immense privileges, and responsibility for the rest of creation.

Let us pray

> O LORD, our Lord,
> how majestic is thy name in all the earth! . . .
> When I look at thy heavens, the work of thy fingers,
> the moon and the stars which thou hast established;

* *Genesis 1:26–7.*

what is man that thou art mindful of him,
and the son of man that thou dost care for him?
Yet thou hast made him little less than God,
and dost crown him with glory and honour.
Thou hast given him dominion over the works of thy hands;
thou hast put all things under his feet . . .
O LORD, our Lord,
how majestic is thy name in all the earth!†

Amen

† *Psalm 8:1, 3–6, 9.*

Being ourselves

We are shaped by both nature and nurture.

We naturally take after our parents. You may have your mother's nose, or your father's temperament. Don't people always love to see who the new-born baby takes after?

Then there's nurture – the way we're brought up. We're shaped by the attitudes of our parents, our school, our society. We tend to be like the people we're with – to go along with the crowd and accept their values, instead of thinking things out for ourselves. The mass media tell us what we should be like; what we should wear; what music we should enjoy; how to make ourselves attractive.

With all these influences upon us, we must not lose sight of the fact that we are all individuals. There has never been anyone quite like me before, and there never will be again! Even identical twins, with the same parents and upbringing, are each individual persons with their own lives to lead.

But most of us spend our lives playing at being someone else. We try to put across an image of ourselves – the way we'd like other people to see us. It's as if we have masks to wear for different situations: how we'd like our friends to see us – our parents – our teachers. It's hard work making sure the mask doesn't slip.

But the most relaxing people to be with are usually those who are confident enough to just be themselves. You can trust them, because you know they are genuine; you know where you are with them.

Why aren't we all like that, all of the time? Perhaps it comes with maturity. Perhaps we need to try out various images, before we can understand what our true self is like. Or maybe we are ashamed to be ourselves and think that no one will accept us as we are.

It is only when we are loved – not for what we're pretending to be, or what we'd like to be, but for what we really are – that we can accept ourselves and make the best of ourselves.

Let us pray

Dear LORD, you who know our inner thoughts, and feelings, and desires, and yet love us for ourselves.
Help me to discover my true self,
and please give me the courage to be myself.

Amen

Selfish greed

The story of Adam and Eve tells how God made the beautiful Garden of Eden, and put the man and the woman there. He planted lots of trees whose fruit they could eat; but there was one, the tree of the knowledge of good and evil, which was forbidden to them. The story goes on:

> The serpent was more crafty than any wild creature that the LORD God had made. He said to the woman, 'Is it true that God has forbidden you to eat from any tree in the garden?' The woman answered the serpent, 'We may eat the fruit of any tree in the garden, except for the tree in the middle of the garden; God has forbidden us either to eat or to touch the fruit of that; if we do, we shall die.' The serpent said, 'Of course you will not die. God knows that as soon as you eat it, your eyes will be opened and you will be like gods knowing both good and evil.' When the woman saw that the fruit of the tree was good to eat, and that it was pleasing to the eye and tempting to contemplate, she took some and ate it. She also gave her husband some and he ate it. Then the eyes of both of them were opened and they discovered that they were naked; so they stitched fig-leaves together and made themselves loincloths.*

This story from the Bible may be three thousand years old, but there is still a lot of truth in it. We may have come a long way since then, in many respects, but human nature itself doesn't seem to have changed that much. The people who first told this story knew that humankind had lost its innocence. They knew that, even when we have so much, we always want more. They knew that if we're forbidden to have something, that's the one thing we want. The sin of Adam and Eve is called 'original sin', because it refers to the selfish greed which is in all of us to some degree, and which is at the root of all other sins.

* *Genesis 3:1–7.*

Let us pray

LORD, we confess our greed and our selfishness.
Help us to realise that our gain is another's loss,
and to be grateful for all we have.

Amen

Making the best of things

There is a Jewish story which tells of a king who owned an enormous diamond. It was very beautiful and very valuable but, unfortunately, it had a deep scar down one side. It was so precious to the king that he promised to give his daughter in marriage to any man who could repair the fault which spoilt the diamond. Many hopeful suitors tried, but failed. Finally, an artist set to work on it. He made use of the line of the fault for the stem of a beautiful rose, which he engraved on the diamond. In this way, he transformed the ugly scar into a thing of beauty – and so won the hand of the princess.

We are each like that diamond: very precious, very valuable, but by no means perfect. We all have our good and bad sides. The secret of life is in learning to make the best of our faults.

Let us pray

Thank you, LORD, for all that makes me me;
For making me unique.
Thank you for making me special to my parents and friends and all who know me.
Help me to make the most of myself:
Help me to use my mind, my character, my talents and my opportunities
to the very best advantage.

Amen

Don't stare

There was once a teacher who came to school with two odd shoes. I don't mean that she wore two left shoes, or two right shoes, but that she had on two shoes from different pairs. They were both black – at least, one was black and the other a very dark navy. They were quite similar in style; and it wasn't too surprising that she made the mistake as she hurried out of the house to catch the train.

By the time she noticed, it was too late to turn back. She tried to hide one foot behind the other as she sat on the train. But it wasn't so easy once she got to school, unless she was going to hop about and stand on one leg all the time.

She went around all day *convinced* that everyone had noticed, and that everyone was staring at her or whispering about her. And whenever anyone laughed, she felt sure they were laughing at her.

This is just a rather trivial example – and she was able to joke about it afterwards with her friends. But it does highlight how sensitive people can be. We hate the idea of being the odd one out, and of being stared at and made fun of. Even when people are very brash about things – deliberately drawing attention to their oddities – this might be their way of covering up their real feelings of shame and embarrassment.

Think how awful it must be for people who are more severely handicapped than just having two odd shoes. How must *they* feel when, every time they go out, people notice that they are different and sometimes stare and make hurtful remarks?

Let us pray

LORD, there are a lot of things about ourselves which we cannot change and we just have to learn to live with. Help us to realise that everyone is sensitive about their appearance. Help us to accept the way people look, and not cause them embarrassment.

Amen

FORGIVENESS

Guilt

If we are honest, we all know that there are times when we do or say things which we regret. We realise that we were in the wrong, and we feel ashamed of ourselves. How do we cope with these failures and the feeling of guilt that they leave with us?

We could just try to forget about them.
But psychologists tell us that guilt needs to be recognised and dealt with. We can't just forget about it. Even if we manage to put it out of our conscious mind, it will sink down into our subconscious and affect the sort of person we are.

We could try to do better next time.
Certainly we should try, but we all know that this isn't as easy as it sounds. If we have a bad temper, we are likely to fly off the handle the next time we are provoked, however much we regretted it the last time.

We could pray for forgiveness.
Many people find comfort in prayer. 'Comfort' has become a nice, soft, cosy word, but it really means 'with fortitude' or 'with strength'. When people pray for forgiveness, they ask for God's power to give them a clear conscience, and for God's strength to help them overcome their faults in future.

We could go to confession.
In some traditions, people confess their sins out loud to a priest. He acts as God's spokesman and assures people that God has forgiven them. Many people find it helpful to admit their guilt openly in this way. Those who do not go to church may unburden themselves on a counsellor. Many of us probably do it on a good friend.

We could do something to make up for what we did wrong.
If we're really sorry, then of course we'll try to put things right, or make up for it in some way.

Let us pray

Be merciful to me, O GOD, because of your constant love.
Because of your great mercy, wipe away my sins!
Create a pure heart in me, O God,
and put a new and loyal spirit in me.*

Amen

* *Psalm 51:1, 10.*

A fresh start

There are certain times which are ideal for making a fresh start – the coming of spring, for instance. As the trees begin to clothe themselves anew so we put away winter things, and are cheered by the bright colours of summer fashions in the shops. The sunshine reminds us that windows need cleaning and parts of the house need decorating. The warmer weather tempts us out into the fresh air, and people start working on their gardens. Spring-cleaning is a ritual in which we put the long winter months behind us, and look forward to warmer days ahead.

It's not just the house and garden that need to be cleared out occasionally. We need to spring-clean our inner lives, too. We need time to sort ourselves out, throw away all the clutter and clean ourselves up. In other words, deal with those things which have been niggling away at our consciences. We can only clear them out by recognising where we have gone wrong, being sorry and resolving not to repeat it. It would be soul-destroying to be always thinking about our failings but, like spring-cleaning, it's a valuable exercise on regular occasions. Then we can set out again with a clear conscience and a new start.

Let us pray

LORD, help us to make the most of the special breaks
in the routine of our lives.
Times when we can take stock of the past
and turn towards the future.
May we be ready to admit our faults,
to accept forgiveness,
and to start out again on life,
determined always to improve what we can,
and never to despair about what we can't.

Amen

Forgiving others

When people hurt our feelings, it may be difficult for us to forgive and forget. We can't just carry on as though nothing has happened. Perhaps we won't talk to them any more, or try to avoid them altogether. But what does this achieve? Sulking only makes us more miserable; and the longer we nurse a grudge, the bigger it will grow. It's surely better to accept apologies graciously – to forgive and remain friends. Young children seem to realise this, and they have a disarming way of going about it:

> Make up, make up, never, never break up.
> If you do, you'll get the flu,
> and that will be the end of you!

In the New Testament, Jesus gives advice on forgiving others. Peter, the spokesman for the twelve disciples, asked Jesus how many times he should forgive people. He thought he was being generous when he suggested seven times. But Jesus said – not seven times – but seventy times seven! We could never keep count up to 490 times, and what Jesus meant was that we should set no limits on our willingness to forgive – just as we can always turn to God for forgiveness, no matter how many times we do wrong.

The New Testament Letter to the Ephesians says this:

> Let all bitterness and wrath and anger and clamour and slander be put away from you, with all malice, and be kind to one another, tenderhearted, forgiving one another, as God in Christ forgave you.*

Let us pray

FATHER, forgive us our sins as we forgive those who sin against us.
When others have wronged us, may we be ready and willing to put things right, and not make things worse between us.
Help us to be kind and tenderhearted, willing to forgive others as readily as you forgive us.

Amen

* *Ephesians 4:31–2.*

Humility

Lucy says to Charlie Brown:
'You know what the whole trouble with you is, Charlie Brown?'
'No; and I don't want to know! Leave me alone!'
'The whole trouble with you is: you won't listen to what the whole trouble with you is.'

Jesus is famous for his parables that are recorded in the New Testament. He told this one for people who were too conceited to see anything wrong with themselves, and who looked down on everyone else. (The Pharisees of Jesus' day were very religious Jews.)

'Once there were two men who went up to the Temple to pray: one was a Pharisee, the other a tax collector. The Pharisee stood apart by himself and prayed, "I thank you, God, that I am not greedy, dishonest, or an adulterer, like everybody else. I thank you that I am not like that tax collector over there. I fast two days a week and I give you a tenth of all my income." But the tax collector stood at a distance and would not even raise his face to heaven, but beat on his breast and said, "God, have pity on me, a sinner!"

'I tell you,' said Jesus, 'the tax collector, and not the Pharisee, was in the right with God when he went home. For everyone who makes himself great will be humbled, and everyone who humbles himself will be made great.'*

I wonder how Jesus would tell this story today?

Form 3G were at the playing fields for games. In the changing room after the match, Simon was having a laugh with his mates. He was obviously popular. He was the team captain, and a natural sportsman. He was full of himself just now, having scored the winning goal. Then he caught sight of Tom who was changing quietly by himself over in the corner. Tom was the last reserve and hadn't even got on the pitch that day. He knew he was hopeless at football and went red in the face when Simon started to make fun of him in front of the others. Still, Tom was determined to keep trying, and maybe eventually he would get better at it.

* *Luke 18:10–14.*

The trouble is, when we're too full of ourselves, we cannot see our own faults. We're too self-satisfied with the image we present to the outside world to ask ourselves what we are really like inside. And when we cannot see our faults, we are less likely to sympathise with other people and with their short-comings. We can only understand other people's faults when we are able to admit to our own.

Let us pray

LORD, help us not to think too highly of ourselves,
and not to despise others.
Help us to look at ourselves honestly,
to be ready to admit our own faults,
and to show more understanding of other people's.

Amen

LOVE

A definition

When we think of love, loving and being in love, we probably think first and foremost of the love between man and woman – romantic love. But, as Bishop Trevor Huddleston reminds us, love can be defined much more widely than this.

> Love is a relationship based and grounded on self-giving and this creates its own power, its own dynamic thing. When we think that love has got to be restricted to the man/woman relationship in, or out of, marriage, we're making a very big mistake. In fact, I think this is one of the major mistakes of the Permissive Society: it's bunk really.
>
> Love as a relationship can exist in terms of friendship between equals of both sexes, either sex together, and this is a tremendously precious thing, and can be much more creative and powerful than a marriage relationship. Love between a parent and child continuing through life can be enormously creative.
>
> And then of course, for the Christian, at the apex is the love of the creature for his Creator, of man for God. This is a relationship which is infinitely richer than any of the others. It embraces all the others and it fulfils all the others and it often changes all the others, and gives the proper balance to them.
>
> That's my definition of love.

Let us pray

O GOD, who has prepared for them that love thee
such good things as pass man's understanding;
Pour into our hearts such love toward thee,
that we, loving thee above all things, may obtain thy promises,
which exceed all that we can desire.*

Amen

* Collect for the sixth Sunday after Trinity, Book of Common Prayer.

All you need is love

However brash we may be on the surface, all of us are sensitive deep down. Human beings need to be handled with care. We can be easily hurt by the things people say and do to us – or the things they neglect to say or do. Yet we respond when people treat us lovingly. The following extract from Tolstoy expounds this idea further.

> People think there are circumstances when one may deal with human beings without love, but no such circumstances ever exist. Inanimate objects may be dealt with without love: we may fell trees, bake bricks, hammer iron without love. But human beings cannot be handled without love, any more than bees can be handled without care. That is the nature of bees. If you handle bees carelessly you will harm the bees and yourself as well. And so it is with people. And it cannot be otherwise, because mutual love is the fundamental law of human life.
>
> It is true that man cannot force himself to love in the way he can force himself to work, but it does not follow from this that men may be treated without love, especially if something is required from them. If you feel no love – leave people alone. Occupy yourself with things, with yourself, with anything you like, only not with men. Just as one can eat without harm and profitably only when one is hungry, so can one usefully and without injury deal with men only when one loves them. But once a man allows himself to treat men unlovingly, there are no limits to the cruelty and brutality that he may inflict on others.

Let us pray

LORD, help us today, to be aware
of other people's need for love,
just as we need love ourselves.
Help us to remember
that we cannot treat people as objects,
without both them and us becoming less than human.
'Mutual love is the fundamental law of human life.'

Amen

The burning flame

Love is a very powerful force in human relationships. It is a drive within us which, if properly channelled, can be very fulfilling. But anything powerful must be respected. Like a burning flame, it is precious but dangerous.

C.S. Lewis wrote, 'To love at all is to be vulnerable. Love anything and your heart will certainly be wrung and possibly broken.' He goes on to say that if you keep your heart intact, it will become 'unbreakable, impenetrable, irredeemable'.

The passage which follows has a similar message. When you love someone, you are putting yourself at risk, for you can easily be hurt. And when you experience love, you grow in self-knowledge, which also can be painful. But the poet admits that, if you do not allow yourself to love, then you are only half living.

The passage and the prayer are by Kahlil Gibran.

Then said Almitra, Speak to us of Love.
And he raised his head and looked upon the people, and there fell a stillness upon them. And with a great voice he said:
When love beckons you, follow him,
Though his ways are hard and steep.
And when his wings enfold you, yield to him,
Though the sword hidden among his pinions may wound you.
And when he speaks to you believe in him,
Though his voice may shatter your dreams as the north wind lays waste the garden.
For even as love crowns you so shall he crucify you. Even as he is for your growth so he is for your pruning.
. . .
All these things shall love do unto you that you may know the secrets of your heart, and in that knowledge become a fragment of Life's heart.

But if in your fear you would seek only love's peace and love's pleasure,
Then it is better for you that you cover your nakedness and pass out of love's threshing-floor,
Into the seasonless world where you shall laugh, but not all of your laughter, and weep, but not all of your tears.

Let us pray

All life is twain, the one a frozen stream,
the other a burning flame,
And the burning flame is love.

Make me, O Lord, food for the burning flame,
And make me, O God, fuel for the sacred fire.

Amen

Service

What is love? We usually think of it as a feeling, an emotion. But what's the use of love if it's just a nice warm feeling inside – something we sing about in songs, and write about in poetry? Love must be shown in the way we act!

When Jesus told his followers, 'Love one another, as I have loved you,' he also gave them a demonstration of what he meant. This took place at the Last Supper – the night before he died.

> During supper, Jesus, well aware that the Father had entrusted everything to him, and that he had come from God and was going back to God, rose from table, laid aside his garments, and taking a towel, tied it round him. Then he poured water into a basin, and began to wash his disciples' feet and to wipe them with the towel. . . .
>
> After washing their feet and taking his garments again, he sat down. 'Do you understand what I have done for you?' he asked. 'You call me "Master" and "Lord", and rightly so, for that is what I am. Then if I, your Lord and Master, have washed your feet, you also ought to wash one another's feet. I have set you an example: you are to do as I have done for you. . . .
>
> 'I give you a new commandment: love one another; as I have loved you, so you are to love one another.'*

Let us pray

Dear God, the source of all love,
You have shown us that true love consists in serving others,
And commanded us to love each other with your selfless love.
Give us, we pray, that same love
with which Jesus served humanity,
and in which he lived and died.

Love is the doorway through which the human soul passes from selfishness to service, and from solitude to kinship with all mankind.

Amen

* *John 13:3–5, 12–15, 34.*

Love is the greatest

There is a famous New Testament passage in St Paul's first letter to the Corinthians. It speaks of three things which will endure for ever: faith, hope and love – but says the greatest of them all is *love*.

It describes in detail what love is like. Each phrase is worth thinking about:

Love is inexhaustibly patient.
Love anticipates a person's needs and meets them.
Love doesn't mind when someone else has the limelight, responsibilities, popularity or privileges.
Love is not anxious to impress.
Love does not blow its own trumpet.
Love is not aggressive, but courteous.
Love does not insist on its own way.
Love is not touchy, or easily rubbed up the wrong way.
Love keeps no list of the faults and failings of others.
Love doesn't gloat over the mistakes of others in order to put itself in a better light; instead it is glad when others are right.
Love throws a cloak of silence over what is displeasing in other people.
Love trusts that in everything God works for good.
Love looks forward to the future glory promised by God.
Love is not shaken even by the worst of storms.
Love is eternal.

Let us pray

LORD, grant us your love,
That we may rejoice with the glad,
and sympathise with the sad;
That we may always look for the best in people,
and never become too wrapped up with ourselves.
Help us to become more loving,
by sharing our love with others.

Amen

CHARITY

Giving

Ebenezer Scrooge in Dickens' *A Christmas Carol* was a lonely and unhappy man, until he learned the joy of giving. Unfortunately, the Rich Fool in one of Jesus' stories never learned that lesson. He was a farmer who amassed more and more wealth each year, building bigger and bigger barns to store all his grain. Then, when he finally decided that it was time for him to sit back and enjoy it – that very night, he died! His money may have made him the envy of his neighbours, but he was a poor fool in God's eyes. He had thrown away his life on money, never knowing the fulfilment that comes from giving rather than getting, and the pleasure of making other people happy.

People have many different attitudes to what they have and what they give away. How do *we* regard our money? How do we respond when someone asks us to give to charity? Ought we to share our wealth with those in need?

Some say, 'What's mine's mine.' Others enjoy their possessions more if they share them, rather than keeping them to themselves. Some people are very generous, but only to their friends and families. Others feel compassion for people they will never meet and whose names they will never know. Some will only give to those they think deserve it. Others say, 'There, but for the grace of God, go I.' Some will pop a coin in a tin if it is rattled under their noses. Others will think carefully about charities, and make out bankers' orders to support them regularly. Some people give out of a sense of guilt; others out of solidarity with those in need. Some do not just give money, but also their time and efforts to campaign for a fairer society.

Let us pray

Let us think about this poem by Gibran, which also looks at people's motives in giving, and comes to some uncomfortable conclusions:

You give but little when you give of your possessions.
It is when you give of yourself that you truly give.

. . .

There are those who give little of the much which they have –
and they give it for recognition and their hidden desire makes their gifts unwholesome.
And there are those who have little and give it all.
These are the believers in life and the bounty of life, and their coffer is never empty.

. . .

It is well to give when asked, but it is better to give unasked, through understanding.

. . .

You often say, 'I would give, but only to the deserving.'
The trees in your orchard say not so, nor the flocks in your pasture.
They give that they may live, for to withhold is to perish.

. . .

See first that you yourself deserve to be a giver, and an instrument of giving.
For in truth it is life that gives unto life – while you, who deem yourself a giver, are but a witness.

Amen

Be thankful

The New Testament says:

> Command those who are rich in the things of this life . . . to do good, to be rich in good works, to be generous and ready to share with others.*

Most of us do not think of ourselves as rich. We're not millionaires; we don't drive around in a Rolls Royce; and we haven't got a swimming-pool in the back garden. But even if our family has no car and lives in rented accommodation, we would still appear rich to two-thirds of the world's people. The standard of living which we take for granted in this country would seem luxurious to the poor of the Third World.

Perhaps we can appreciate this a little if we have ever had to 'rough it'. Perhaps, after a camping holiday, we have been thankful to get back to a dry house, a hot bath and a comfortable bed. Or we may have known hard times: when there wasn't enough money at the end of the week to buy food; when we've had to make do with hand-me-downs instead of new and fashionable clothes; and when there were no big presents at Christmas.

But even so, the situation for most people in the Third World is much worse.

> [When volunteer helpers return from the Third World] many experience immediate euphoria when they realise that they can again drink the water, have a rest, see green grass and not have to steel themselves to incessant death. [But] the relief does not last long: 'After about a week,' one man explains, 'the guilt begins; you wonder how you can bear to be part of such a selfish society.'
>
> No one understands what they have been through. A gap separates them from friends and relatives. Jane Robertson, a nurse with Save the Children Fund, back in England after six months, found herself peering, appalled, into the boot of her sister's car: a day's outing with two small children seemed to require more than the possessions of an entire Ethiopian family.

* *1 Timothy 6:17–18.*

Let us pray

LORD, help us to appreciate how rich we really are:
in having food to eat and water fit to drink;
in having a roof over our heads, and clothes to wear;
in having education, and medical facilities,
and families and friends to care for us.
Help us not to take these things for granted,
and not to waste the good things we have;
but 'to be rich in good works, to be generous
and ready to share with others.'

Amen

Disaster funds

It has been claimed that the mid-eighties saw one of the greatest natural disasters of historic times. Drought, sweeping across the northern part of Africa, drove people from their homes, killed off their livestock and claimed innumerable human lives. The pitiful images of men, women and children dying of starvation were brought to our television screens in October 1985 – and the public's generous response was immediate and overwhelming.

It is chilling to learn that this disaster was known about well over a year before those harrowing reports intruded into our living rooms. And by the time the British public was informed, it was almost too late to take effective action. Why hadn't we heard about it sooner? Simply because it was not considered a good enough story. Disasters abroad, which do not affect our own people, have to be pretty dramatic before they hit the news headlines.

What is even more disturbing is that, during the African crisis of 1985 to 87, more children died in India and Pakistan than in all 46 nations of Africa put together.* But who wants to hear of the ceaseless, grinding poverty in the Third World? Of the silent disaster of malnutrition and disease which carries off 40,000 children every day around the world?†

It is a sad comment on human nature that our interest has to be captured by exciting news items before we will react to human suffering. That we will give to disaster funds rather than to those charities which are working on long-term development projects designed to avert such disasters. That we will give to children's charities rather than to alleviate the pressing problems of the elderly, of prisoners and their families or of drug addicts. Full-scale disasters appeal, but lives lived out in quiet misery do not.

* *UNICEF report, The State of the World's Children*, 1987.
† OXFAM leaflet, *Hunger: The World Picture.*

Let us pray

LORD, open our eyes, our hearts and our minds,
to sympathise with those who suffer,
and to understand the work of the organisations which help them.
If we want to give, may we be open-handed in our generosity,
not just in emergencies, but also in supporting on-going development projects.

Amen

World hunger

When we look back at the Western world in the nineteenth century, we are horrified at some of the things that went on. How could 'good Christian people' allow slavery, for instance? How could they justify the suffering caused by capturing Africans from their homes – transporting them to America in such crowded conditions that many did not survive the voyage – and then buying and selling them as if they were objects to be possessed and used, rather than human beings to be respected?

Just as we now look back on slavery in amazement and disgust, will people in the future look back at us and wonder how we could allow so many human beings to die of starvation at a time when there were world food surpluses? And will they look back in disbelief at the communication problems in getting food to the needy, when we have the technology to send people to the moon?

It is so easy to accept the situations in which we grow up, and think that they cannot be changed. But if we are to be responsible citizens, we must question the morality of what society does in our name. Slavery was only abolished because of campaigners who spoke out against the cruelty, and refused to be put off. Let us hope that enough of us will be concerned with the food crisis that the governments of the world will unite in a concerted effort to give every human being a fair share of the earth's resources. Let us hope that, by the twenty-first century, people will look back on starvation as a thing of the past.

Let us pray

Our prayer is a meditation on some of the excuses made for hunger:

I was hungry and you blamed it on the Communists.
I was hungry and you circled the moon.
I was hungry and you told me to wait.
I was hungry and you set up a commission.
I was hungry and you said, 'So were my ancestors.'

I was hungry and you said, 'We don't employ men over 45.'
I was hungry and you said, 'God helps those who . . .'
I was hungry and you told me that I shouldn't be.
I was hungry and you told be that machines do that work now.
I was hungry and you had wars to pay for.
I was hungry and you said, 'The poor are always with us.'

LORD, may we no longer accept excuses.

Amen

ONE WORLD

The brotherhood of man

When the Pope was on a tour of African countries in August 1986, he addressed a gathering of one hundred thousand people in the city of Douala in Cameroun. More than 60 per cent of the population of this city is under the age of 21; and the Pope addressed himself to the young people. He said that the youth of today want 'Peace . . . fraternal solidarity without restrictions of race and frontiers. They want to unite in order to overcome hunger in the world.'

It is good that the younger generation does have such ideals – the survival of the human race depends upon them. 'Fraternal solidarity' means identifying with other people, just as if they were our brothers. Humanists argue that we all belong to the human family and are therefore responsible for our 'brothers and sisters' wherever they are in the world. Just as we would not ignore the needs of our own family at home – neither should we be indifferent to the needs of the whole human family.

Religious people would go even further than this. They link this principle of the 'brotherhood of man' to that of the 'Fatherhood of God'. This reading explains:

> One God reigns over all the nations of the world and has pleasure in all his children. In the eyes of the Creator all his children are equal; his goodness is poured forth on all. He does not favour this nation or that nation; all alike are his creatures.
>
> This being so, why should *we* make divisions, separating one race from another? Why should we create barriers of superstition and tradition, bringing discord and hatred among the people?
>
> All peoples and nations are one family, the children of the one Father, and should be to one another as brothers and sisters! If all men were obedient to this principle, the greatest unity and understanding would be established in the hearts of mankind.

Let us pray

LORD and FATHER of us all,
strengthen the bond between all your children;
teach us a deeper understanding of brotherhood,
and bring us to a new unity of love.

Amen

United Nations

The last World War ended in 1945. That year, 51 nations came together to try to find another way of settling their differences apart from armed conflict. The United Nations headquarters in New York now provide a meeting place for representatives of its 153 members states and of nearly every other country in the world. Here issues of international concern are discussed and voted on.

In 1948 the UN adopted the *Universal Declaration of Human Rights*; and this has become the model for the constitutions of many new countries. The first three Articles are as follows:

1. All human beings are born free and equal in dignity and rights. They are endowed with reason and conscience and should act towards one another in a spirit of brotherhood.
2. Everyone is entitled to all the rights and freedoms set forth in this Declaration, without distinction of any kind, such as race, colour, sex, language, religion, political or other opinion, national or social origin, property, birth or other status.
3. Everyone has the right to life, liberty and security of person.

In all, there are 30 Articles of Human Rights; and these are not limited just to our rights, but also speak of our responsibilities. Number 29 says:

> Everyone has duties to the community, in which alone the full and free development of his personality is possible.

These Human Rights are seen by the United Nations as the foundation of freedom, justice and peace in the world. How long will it be before all this is achieved?

Let us pray

LORD GOD, FATHER of all humanity, help us to realise that we belong to the whole human community, and are citizens of the world. Help us to think about and appreciate human rights; and to accept the responsibilities which they imply. May we be willing to work for the day when they will be the birthright of every human being.

Amen

Racial harmony

The reading is from a story about racial tension and racial harmony. It is set in Britain, and the main character is a young artist of West Indian origin.

We strolled round the streets, at home amongst the black-and-white crowds, passing women in saris, black-robed Greeks, ladies wearing bright tie-heads, swaying their hips as they walked. This is what I wanted to paint, what I saw, and I saw a bright world of many colours. I could not join with those who wanted different communities to live in separate [homelands]. It seemed to me that, however unwillingly, cultures *were* mixing. I heard it in the drumbeat of white punk groups. Melodies influenced by Indian and Japanese music were featuring on 'Top of the Pops'. The textile students at College borrowed designs from the prints of Asia and Africa. It was impossible to live in a city and be unaware of Eastern, African and Caribbean costumes, of other languages, of foreign foods.

A rainbow was stretching behind the mouldering houses, lightening the sky with a faint newness. . . . The air was still fresh and untainted after the rain. . . . 'See how beautiful the rainbow is. It's a good luck sign. And look, I've just thought. It's made up of many colours, from pale pink to deep violet, all merging into each other.'

I wanted to share my view of the world. I've always had an artist's eye for colour; fascinated rather than threatened by the different skin tones around me. . . . The different colours of the population were a gift to me, and I thought that it must be really boring to live in a monotone area where everyone was black or white or brown.

Let us pray

LORD GOD, you who 'made of one blood all nations of men', help us to appreciate all the advantages of living in a multi-racial society; and may our differences enrich rather than divide us.

Amen

One truth

> There is a Hindu story which tells of five blind men who lived in an Indian village. One day a prince set an elephant in front of them. He told each one of them to feel the animal and tell him what the elephant was like. The first, who felt its foot, said the elephant was like a pillar. The second, who had touched its ear, said, 'No, it's like a fan.' 'Nonsense,' said the third, who had felt its tusks, 'it's round, hard and smooth like a handle of a plough.' The fourth had felt its tail, and was sure it was a rope. 'Don't be daft,' said the fifth, who had felt its trunk, 'the elephant is like a snake.' So they began to argue among themselves. Each of them was sure that his description of the elephant was right, but although each of them had some idea, none of them knew what the elephant was really like.

In the same way, we all have our own perceptions of the truth; but we need to respect each other and listen to other people's points of view if we are to make proper sense of life.

Religion helps people in their search for truth. But, like the five Indians and the elephant, religions have often come to different conclusions, and have been a divisive factor in the world. There have been wars, not just between one religion and another, but between different denominations of the same religion. Thankfully, nowadays, religions are coming together in dialogue, to try to find their common ground.

The following quotation comes from the Baha'i Faith. This is one of the newest of the world's religions, and one which is very concerned to bring people back together again. It preaches the oneness of God, the oneness of religion, and the oneness of humanity. It believes that there is truth to be found in all religions; and its message is that this truth is able to unite a divided world.

> When you meet those whose opinions differ from your own, do not turn away your face from them. All are seeking truth and there are many roads leading thereto. Truth has many aspects, but it remains always and forever one. Do not allow differences of opinion to separate you from your fellow-men, or to be the cause of dispute, hatred and strife in your hearts. Rather, search diligently for the truth and make all men your friends.

Let us pray

LORD, it is good that we should search
for what is right and what is true;
but give us the humility to recognise
that we shall never know the whole truth;
and guard our keen convictions
from becoming narrow bigotry.

Amen

PEACE

Peace be with you

'Peace be with you' is a greeting which is found in many religions. In church, the priest says, 'The peace of the Lord be always with you'; Muslims say 'Assalamu alaikum'; the Jewish word for peace is Shalom; and the Hindu word is Shanti.

Each of these words for peace does not describe a lack of noise and conflict so much as a positive state of harmony, well-being and fulfilment.

This poem, by Brian Wren, is making the same point: that peace is joy and laughter, rather than the sinister 'peace and quiet' which covers up fear and resentment.

> Say NO to PEACE
> if what they mean by 'peace'
> is the quiet misery of hunger,
> the frozen stillness of fear,
> the silence of broken spirits,
> the unborn hopes of the oppressed.
>
> Tell them that PEACE
> is the shouting of children at play,
> the babble of tongues set free,
> the thunder of dancing feet,
> and a father's voice singing.

We cannot be truly at peace with ourselves and with others simply by avoiding conflicts; by putting up with things, when we know they could be better; by keeping quiet about things which annoy us, simply to avoid a row; by ignoring injustice because 'it's none of our business'. True peace and harmony come from being honest with ourselves and with others: from bringing things out into the open – because only then can conflicts be resolved.

Let us pray

Go forth into the world in peace; be of good courage; hold fast that which is good; render to no man evil for evil; strengthen the faint-hearted; support the weak; help the afflicted; honour all men; love and serve the Lord, rejoicing in the power of the Holy Spirit.

And the peace of the LORD be always with us.

Amen

A better way

We hear a great deal in the news about the violence in South Africa and Northern Ireland, whose societies have for a long time been tearing themselves apart, and where innocent people suffer simply because of their colour or their creed. In both countries children have grown up in the midst of conflict not knowing the meaning of peace. Many people can see no way out of the problems, and can only predict further bloodshed. But in both situations there are beacons of hope, signalling a better way.

In Northern Ireland, for instance, there is Corrymeela. The name means Hill of Harmony, and it is a Christian centre where Catholics and Protestants are brought together. Here the barriers of prejudice and suspicion are gradually broken down as they get to know each other as people – without the labels society pins on them. It is true that, afterwards, they must return to their separate communities, but the experience of Corrymeela cannot be taken away from them – the experience of reconciliation across the sectarian divide.

And what about South Africa? In 1987 missionary doctors Maggie and Anthony Barker returned to South Africa after twelve years. During their absence relationships between black and white people had got worse, and resistance to the government had hardened among the black people who are in the majority but denied the right to vote. The Barkers – as white people – did not know what to expect when they returned to the hospital at Nqutu, where they had worked for thirty years. They take up the story:

> What we had not anticipated was the mass of people round the hospital gate, nor the hands that reached out to touch our hands, shaking them again and again. . . . This was the flip side to the revolution. Instead of sternness we were being swamped by love. It was totally inexplicable; totally humbling. . . . Was this the way Africa forgave you your many sins? . . . We had a dream there once, at Nqutu, of people brought closer together in a kind of practical loving. It worked out in the lecture room and the operating theatre, the labour wards, the chapel, in baseball games on Sunday afternoons and graduation ceremonies for successful nurses. Still this seems a better way into the future than the way South

Africa is headed now. There are unmistakable signs at Nqutu that the vision has not entirely faded. God grant that it stays bright for them.

Let us pray

LORD, we ask you to continue to inspire people with the vision of hope in the midst of despair; with the vision of peace in the midst of violence; and of reconciliation when two sides are locked in conflict. Grant that this vision of a better way stays bright for our brothers and sisters in Northern Ireland and South Africa.

Amen

Strength to love

Mahatma Gandhi in India and Martin Luther King in the United States of America were the greatest spokesmen for peace of the twentieth century. Although they resisted the evils which they saw in society, they refused to fight evil with evil. They practised non-violent resistance, believing that it is always wrong to use violence, even in self-defence. Yet both these men of peace met violent deaths. They remind us that pacifism is not for weaklings, but demands courage, strength, self-restraint and faith. For both Gandhi and King knew that their lives were in danger from those who disagreed with them, but they would not be deflected from their purpose.

We live in a world which equates power with the force of arms. Both Gandhi and King believed in a greater force – the power of love. They argued that violence only ever leads to destruction, but love can reform society. In this passage, Martin Luther King speaks of his faith in this 'soul force' – the power of love. It is clear that, for him, love was not 'sentimental and anaemic', but a force to be reckoned with:

> Somehow we must be able to stand up before our most bitter opponents and say: 'We shall match your capacity to inflict suffering by our capacity to endure suffering. We will meet your physical force with soul force. Do to us what you will and we will still love you. . . . But be assured that we'll wear you down by our capacity to suffer, and one day we will win our freedom. We will not only win freedom for ourselves, we will so appeal to your heart and conscience that we will win you in the process, and our victory will be a double victory.'

Let us pray

Since the early 1980s, this Prayer for Peace has been used all over the world by those who sincerely believe that physical force can be met by soul force:

Lead me from death to life, from falsehood to truth.
Lead me from despair to hope, from fear to trust.
Lead me from hate to love, from war to peace.
Let peace fill our heart, our world, our universe.

Amen

Turn the other cheek

How do you react to this advice?

> 'Love your enemies; do good to those who hate you; bless those who curse you; pray for those who treat you spitefully. When a man hits you on the cheek, offer him the other cheek too; when a man takes your coat, let him have your shirt as well. Give to everyone who asks you; when a man takes what is yours, do not demand it back. Treat others as you would like them to treat you.'*

Like a lot of Jesus' teaching in the New Testament, it seems to stand normal human values on their head. If someone hits us, isn't it natural to strike back? If someone is rude to us, isn't it natural to answer back? If someone is nasty to us in some way, don't we want to get our own back?

Yet we must admit that, if we always try to get our own back, the matter doesn't usually stop there. It usually gets worse. This is how Martin Luther King saw it:

> The ultimate weakness of violence is that it is a descending spiral, begetting the very thing it seeks to destroy. Instead of diminishing evil, it multiplies it. . . . Through violence you murder the hater, but you do not murder hate. In fact, violence merely increases hate . . . Returning violence for violence multiplies violence, adding deeper darkness to a night already devoid of stars. Darkness cannot drive out darkness; only light can do that. Hate cannot drive out hate; only love can do that.

Let us pray

The prayer of St Francis:

> Lord, make us instruments of your peace.
> Where there is hatred, let us sow love;
> Where there is injury, pardon;
> Where there is discord, union;
> Where there is doubt, faith;

* *Luke 6:28–31.*

Where there is despair, hope;
Where there is darkness, light;
Where there is sadness, joy;
For your mercy and for your truth's sake.

Amen

Remembrance

The eleventh hour of the eleventh day of the eleventh month was the official ending of the First World War. So Remembrance Sunday is always the Sunday nearest to the 11th of November. On that day, poppies are worn and wreaths of poppies are laid at memorials. They are a reminder of the fields of poppies in northern France where many soldiers were killed in the First World War, and where large military cemeteries now mark their burial places. On that day, many people keep two minutes' silence out of respect for the dead of the two World Wars and of the more recent Falklands Campaign.

There is, of course, a danger in remembering war. The uniforms, the medals, the drills, the display of arms and the patriotic tunes can lead to the glorifying of war. But not only is there a danger in remembering war – for those of us who have not experienced war, there is a danger of forgetting. A danger of forgetting the horror and suffering of war: the millions of young soldiers who met their deaths prematurely; the wholesale destruction of all that people had lovingly built up; the cost – the waste – the loss – the fear and the pain. Many people still live with the scars of war, both physical and mental.

Today, in our nuclear age, it is even more important to think about the consequences of war – however much we would like to forget it and pretend that the nuclear threat does not exist. The Chernobyl disaster in 1985 gave us just a glimpse of the devastation which could follow a nuclear holocaust – of how innocent people would automatically become involved, and the earth's atmosphere poisoned.

If Remembrance Sunday reminds us of the tragedy of war, then perhaps it will help us to keep the peace.

Let us pray

Wilfred Owen was a soldier in the First World War, who was killed in France just before the war ended in 1918. He was twenty-five years old – and he shared the destiny of millions of other young men on both sides. But, unlike most of them, he had the sensibility to see what war really meant, and the power to put this into poetry. Our prayer is taken from one of his poems:

> Be slowly lifted up, thou long black arm,
> Great gun towering towards Heaven, about to curse;
> . . .
> Reach at that arrogance which needs thy harm,
> And beat it down before its sins grow worse;
> . . .
> But when thy spell be cast complete and whole,
> May God curse thee, and cut thee from our soul!

Amen

SUFFERING

Why?

One of the biggest stumbling blocks to religious belief is the problem of suffering. 'How can we believe in God,' people ask, 'when such terrible things happen in the world?'

If God exists, and he is good, loving and all-powerful, why does he allow us to suffer?

There are many answers that can be given to this dilemma. In the following passage, by Abdul Baha of the Baha'i religion, two major ideas are put forward. The first is self-evident and accounts for a great deal of human suffering:

> If a person eats too much, he ruins his digestion. If he takes poison, he becomes ill or dies. If a person gambles, he will lose his money; if he drinks too much, he will lose his balance. All these sufferings are caused by the person himself. It is quite clear therefore that certain sorrows are the result of our own deeds.

The second is a religious idea, which tries to make sense of the fact that innocent people suffer also:

> Other sufferings there are which come upon the Faithful of God. Consider the great sorrows endured by Christ and by his apostles. Those who suffer most, attain to the greatest perfection. . . .While a person is happy, he may forget his God; but when grief comes and sorrows overwhelm him, then will he remember his Father who is in Heaven, and who is able to deliver him. People who do not suffer, attain no perfection. The plant most pruned by the gardeners is the one which, when the summer comes, will have the most beautiful blossoms and the most abundant fruit.

Let us pray

LORD, we pray for all whom we know who are suffering, in any way, at this time. We pray that they will not be destroyed by their suffering, but find inner strength to come through it; and that they may become better people because of it. We ask that we also may be given courage to face suffering when it comes our way.

Amen

The point of pain

Religious people often wonder why God made the world with so much pain and suffering. An answer comes when we think what life would be like if we could not feel pain.

The following passage was written by Brother Carlo Carretto, when he was working in Hong Kong, and thinking about a drug addict whom he had recently helped.

> Never had the purpose of pain in man's life struck me so forcibly.
>
> What would become of man without the effects of physical pain?
>
> What would stop him?
>
> What would warn him that he was harming himself?
>
> What would show him the consequences of his excesses? Of the wounds he was inflicting on his nature?
>
> Man is free to indulge in riotous living and to live by overthrowing the order of things, but on his way he will surely meet the suffering that will prostrate him. . . .
>
> I am reminded of the story of Pinocchio. He is made of wood, so is insensitive to pain. But when he let his leg loll in the fireplace near the fire, his insensitivity to pain became a great danger and threatened his life.
>
> It seems absurd to say it, but: what would happen if there were no pain to sensitize us in time, to warn us?
>
> What would have stopped the junkie of last night?
>
> What would warn the alcoholic of the disorder in which he lives?
>
> Man is so sick with sin, so thirsty for pleasure, that if there were no hedge of pain he would soon become satanic.
>
> Nothing would interfere with his desires.
>
> He would be perfectly prepared to trample over dead bodies if only he could satisfy his requirements.

Let us pray

LORD, we thank you for our physical nature
which makes us shrink from pain.
Give us the good sense to take pain as a warning,
so that we avoid the things which cause it,
and try to live in harmony with nature.

Amen

A challenge

Perhaps we dream of a world without suffering. But what would it really be like? The following exchange of views, from Aldous Huxley's novel *Brave New World*, suggests that there is positive value in suffering. The **Controller** discusses the convenient, comfortable, stable, sterile New World with the **Savage**, who represents the old. The Savage finds no challenge in this Brave New World:

C: In a properly organised society like ours, nobody has any opportunities for being noble or heroic. Conditions have got to be thoroughly unstable before the occasion can arise. Where there are wars, where there are divided allegiances, where there are temptations to be resisted, objects of love to be fought for or defended – there, obviously, nobility and heroism have some sense. But there aren't any wars nowadays. The greatest care is taken to prevent you from loving anyone too much. There's no such thing as a divided allegiance; you're so conditioned that you can't help doing what you ought to do. And what you ought to do is on the whole so pleasant . . . that there really aren't any temptations to resist. . . .

S: What you need is something with tears for a change. Nothing costs enough here. . . .

C: We prefer to do things comfortably.

S: But I don't want comfort. I want God, I want poetry, I want real danger, I want freedom, I want goodness. I want sin.

C: In fact, you're claiming the right to be unhappy.

S: All right, then, I'm claiming the right to be unhappy.

Let us pray

LORD, when we suffer, may we be tested and strengthened by it. May it leave us more reflective, with deepened emotions and heightened sensitivity to others. May we come through our suffering as greater individuals.

Amen

Other people's suffering

In the rush and bustle of everyday life it's very easy to be blind to the suffering of others – even of people amongst whom we live.

The poet, W.H. Auden, reflects on this as he looks at the painting by Brueghel, called *Icarus*.

Icarus was a character from a Greek myth. He and his father Daedalus were unjustly imprisoned on the island of Crete, and escaped by making wings of feathers stuck together with wax. When they were ready to fly away, Daedalus warned his son not to fly too low, where the sea would dampen the wings, and not too high, where the sun would melt them. And so they escaped. But the boy became too confident, and flew higher and higher, forgetting his father's warnings. The sun melted the wax, the boy plunged into the sea and, when Daedalus looked down, he saw only feathers floating on the surface.

About suffering they were never wrong,
The Old Masters: how well they understood
Its human position; how it takes place
While someone else is eating or opening a window or just walking dully
along;
. . .
They never forgot
That even the dreadful martyrdom must run its course
Anyhow in a corner, some untidy spot
Where the dogs go on with their doggy life and the torturer's horse
Scratches its innocent behind on a tree.

In Brueghel's *Icarus*, for instance: how everything turns away
Quite leisurely from the disaster; the ploughman may
Have heard the splash, the forsaken cry,
But for him it was not an important failure; the sun shone
As it had to on the white legs disappearing into the green
Water; and the expensive delicate ship that must have seen
Something amazing, a boy falling out of the sky,
Had somewhere to go to and sailed calmly on.

Let us pray

LORD, please help us to be more sensitive to other people's sufferings.
Help us to notice when friends are particularly quiet and withdrawn;
To listen when they mention things which could be worrying them;
To sympathise with their feelings;
And to find ways to help them.

Amen

Every cloud has a silver lining

There's a saying, 'Every cloud has a silver lining.' This reflects the view of life of the optimist: the person who always looks on the bright side of life; who takes some pleasure even in the dullest of daily routines; and who finds some comfort even amid hardships.

People like this show us one way of coping with suffering. They also offer a possible explanation for it. For they see both happiness and suffering as necessary ingredients of human life. Suffering, looked at on its own, may perplex us – like a discord in a piece of music, or an ugly brushstroke on a canvas. But if only we could 'see the whole picture', then perhaps it would all make sense.

This idea is found in these words of William Blake:

Joy and woe are woven fine,
A clothing for the soul divine;
Under every grief and pine
Runs a joy with silken twine.
It is right it should be so;
Man was made for joy and woe;
And when this we rightly know,
Thro' the world we safely go.

Let us pray

LORD, please help us to look for the silver lining
in even the darkest cloud,
that we may never be overwhelmed
either by personal suffering,
or by knowledge of the world's pains.
Give us courage to accept what must be;
strength to bring victory out of disaster,
and time for our hurts to be healed.

Amen

GOOD AND EVIL

Goodies and baddies

> Owen of Clun. He was a huge, powerfully built man with long black hair, a black beard and black eyes that were tunnels into a soul of the same colour. . . . Out of the corner of his eye, Robin could see the portcullis bearing down on the single tree-trunk. With every second that passed, the wood was cracking and giving way. At any moment the whole thing would come crashing down – and he was right underneath it. And Owen's dagger was inching ever closer to his head . . . With a last, desperate effort, Robin pushed Owen away . . . The tree-trunk broke. The portcullis fell. Owen was right underneath it.
>
> A ton of metal with rusting, pointed teeth thundered into the Marcher lord, hurling him to the ground and almost cutting him in two. For a moment he gazed upwards, death and defeat stark in his eyes . . . Trapped behind the portcullis . . . Gulnar raised his hands to the sky, his eyes squirming like maggots in his skull. 'A curse on you, Robin of Sherwood!' he shouted.

A gruesome death. But we breathe a sigh of relief that the evil Owen of Clun can do no more harm. The legendary Robin Hood was 'feared by the bad, loved by the good'.

In real life, people are not usually so easily labelled. We are all capable of both good and evil. We have some good characteristics and some bad ones. Sometimes, in some situations, we are 'very very good', and at other times we are 'horrid'. Sometimes we even find it difficult to know what is right and what is wrong. And other times, when we do good, we're not sure if we do it for the right reasons. Life is very complicated! The important thing is that we don't give up the struggle between good and evil, which goes on within us.

Let us pray

Help us, LORD, to know what is right,
and give us the will-power to do it.

Amen

St George

You may sometimes see a flag flying with a red cross on a white background. It is the flag of St George. Some years ago the Roman Catholic Church struck off St George from its list of saints because so little is known about him as a historical figure. The most a historian can say is that he seems to have been a Christian soldier in the Roman army, who was martyred for his faith in the fourth century. He became popular with the English during the Crusades of the eleventh century, when the red cross of St George was adopted by King Richard the Lionheart. It became the flag of England and was later incorporated into the Union Jack.

Many legends surround St George. The most famous, of course, tells how he slew the dragon. The people of a certain town had been forced to give this dragon two sheep each day for his dinner. When they ran out of sheep, the dragon made do with people instead. George arrived on the very day when it was the turn of the king to sacrifice his lovely daughter to the dragon. George gallantly came to the rescue, and destroyed the terrible monster.

Obviously we don't believe in dragons these days. But even if we know little about the real person behind the legends of St George, these stories can still teach us something. They speak to us of the importance of courage in the face of danger; of a soldier's self-discipline; of taking risks for what you know is right; of putting others before yourself; of the victory of good over evil.

Who knows what dragons we are likely to meet in life, and what battles we may have to fight? When we are confronted with demanding tasks, difficult relationships, personal tragedies, and inner temptations – we can take our inspiration from St George, and face the future with courage and self-discipline, determined to do what we believe to be right.

Let us pray

Teach us, good LORD, to serve you as you deserve:
to give and not to count the cost;
to fight and not to heed the wounds;
to toil and not to seek for rest;
to labour and not to ask for any reward
save that of knowing that we do your will.

Amen

St Michael

You probably know that the purple flowers which come out at the end of September are called Michaelmas Daisies. This is because the 29th September is St Michael's Day, or Michaelmas.

Many churches are dedicated to this saint, including Coventry Cathedral, which has a huge statue of him by Epstein on the outside wall. And St Michael's Mount in Cornwall is named after him, because someone saw a vision of the saint there.

St Michael was not a man – like most of the saints from the Bible – but an angel. The Book of Revelation in the New Testament describes a vision in which the Archangel Micheal defeats the forces of evil:

> Then war broke out in heaven. Michael and his angels waged war upon the dragon. The dragon and his angels fought, but they had not the strength to win, and no foothold was left them in heaven. So the great dragon was thrown down, that serpent of old that led the whole earth astray, whose name is Satan, or the Devil.*

This vision is a dream which many people hold on to: that one day good will overcome evil; and that victory is ultimately assured to those whose cause is just and who stand up for what is right. There is still a struggle going on between good and evil in our world today, and the story of St Michael and his angels encourages people to believe that the struggle is worthwhile.

St Michael is usually portrayed by artists as a soldier, wearing armour, and defeating the devil. This armour can be thought of symbolically as the armour of God: the inner strength of truth and peace and love with which we can face up to evil. St Paul describes this armour in the Letter to the Ephesians; and the following prayer is an adaptation of that passage.

* *Revelation 12:7–9.*

Let us pray

Help us, LORD, to find our strength in you
and in your mighty power.
May we put on the armour which you provide,
so that we can stand firm against evil:
– the belt of truth,
– the chain-mail of integrity,
– the shoes of the gospel of peace, for a firm footing.
Help us to take up the great shield of faith,
to ward off the flaming arrows of the evil one.
Give us salvation as a helmet,
and for our sword, inspire us with your words,
that we may overcome evil with goodness,
and conquer in the power of love and peace.*

Amen

* *Adapted from Ephesians 6:10–17.*

First the bad news

Most of us get to know the daily news. We either watch it on television, listen to it on the radio, read it in the newspapers, or hear about it from our friends.

It is often very depressing, even shocking, especially when accompanied by pictures in full colour on our television screens. The world seems to be a really dreadful place to live in sometimes. I don't just mean the world news either: telling of wars and revolutions, hijacks and bombings, volcanoes and earthquakes. We can come much nearer home. There are plenty of examples of 'man's inhumanity to man' on our own doorsteps:

- The child who accepts an offer of a lift home, and is assaulted.
- The football hooligans who go on the rampage.
- The old people, murdered in their homes by a maniac.

We could go on – the list is endless.

How do we react to all this?

There are those who sometimes find the news too much to bear – and they switch it off. They would rather not know.

There are those who despair of the world in which we live. They become suspicious of everyone, frightened for their own safety, and over-protective towards their children.

It is a pity that 'no news is good news'. That we hear more about the evil in the world than the good.

But it's worth considering that many horrifying things are done by individuals or small groups of people. If *they* can *ruin* the world, then *we*, as individuals or together with our families and friends, have got just as much power to *improve* the world.

Let us pray

LORD, help us never to give in to the evil which sometimes shakes our trust in humanity. May we always be on the lookout for ways in which we can do good, that we may help to make this world a better place to live in.

Amen

BELIEFS

God

For most of our lives, we do not think about the process of breathing in and breathing out, which we are doing all the time. Yet we know that, without oxygen, we would quickly die.

Is God something like the air on which our lives depend, but which we take for granted? If God exists, then he is the source of life, and we cannot live without him. Many people when pressed, will say that they believe in God – and yet they ignore him for most of the time.

People usually only think about breathing when they are having difficulty with it – when, for some reason, they are gasping for breath. In the same way, people often take no notice of God until some crisis occurs. Then they cry out to God for help. But if God exists, he is there all the time, and able to help us in all that we do.

A monk speaks of his own experience of God:

I have never had any difficulty in feeling God's presence, especially when I was small. Rather, his absence would have seemed very strange and very unlikely.

I felt myself to be in God
like a bird in the air
like a log in the fire
like a baby in its mother's womb.

This experience of God's presence in all things and in every situation is not only mine, it belongs to the People of God, that is to say to those who believe.

But let us understand each other: it is not a matter of establishing the union with God on our side. Because that union exists; it already existed before I was aware of it.

What matters on our side is to become aware of this union.

It is the story of the baby who gradually discovers its mother and father. But the mother and father were there already.

And God was there already. It is for us to discover him within ourselves, not to create him.

God's presence in ourselves, in the Cosmos, in the Invisible, in Everything is basic. You will never be in any place, in any situation, where he is not.

Let us pray

LORD GOD, in whom we live and move and have our being,
we take you for granted like the air we breathe,
but without you there would be no life.
Help us to know you,
to be aware of your presence with us,
and to trust in your help.

Amen

Experience

How do you know if somebody loves you? Love is not something that can be seen, or measured, or tested in the laboratory. Yet the love of our parents and friends is something in which we trust because of our experience. In the same way, the existence of God cannot be proved (or disproved) by the scientist. Yet religious feelings are common human experiences: the feelings of awe and wonder at the world in which we live; the inspiration that comes to us 'out of the blue'; the sense of being guided in an important decision; the certainty that we have found our vocation, or purpose in life.

Those who believe in God and live their lives as though in his presence, are living by faith. But their faith is justified in their own experience. This is shown in the following two passages, written by people from different religions:

> I was born a Muslim and have always practised as a Muslim. The significant thing about Islam is that it deals with every aspect of life – with the food you eat, and the way you deal with people. Praying five times a day makes you aware that you are in the eye of God every day. You can't help the feeling of hypocrisy if you go to prayer and then do wrong.

A fifty-year-old Christian, a member of the Baptist Church, says this:

> Going through life, you are always going to have struggles. I don't know how anyone can make it through without faith. To me, going to church every week is like taking in food to feast on for the rest of the week. My burdens are still here, but I can find the strength to carry on. Without faith, I don't know what I would do.

Let us pray

LORD, it is not easy to believe in you
in a society which turns its back on God.
Help us to know your presence in our lives
and to learn to trust ourselves to you.
Amen

Images of God

What image do you have of God? Whether or not you believe in God, you must have some idea of what God is like. If you believe in God – what is it that you believe in? If you don't believe in God – what is it that you are rejecting?

Is your image of God the old-man-in-the-sky of the *Private Eye* cartoons? The Father Christmas figure with a long, white beard, looking down from a cloud? It was an image like this which led the Russians to say they had *proof* that God does not exist. They were the first to put a man into space and, after having a good look round up there, he announced that God was nowhere to be seen!

That is a warning to us not to take our images of God too literally. For no serious thinker would really expect God to be a physical human being living in a material place. God is believed to exist beyond time and space. But, as physical beings ourselves, it is impossible for us to imagine what that means, because our whole lives are controlled by time and space. We cannot imagine what it must be like to live, without living *somewhere*. And the idea of eternity: of having no beginning and no end – is just mind-blowing. So we must continue to have our images of God, but to recognise that they are *only* images – only our feeble human attempts to describe God.

One very popular image is of God as Father. The most important Christian prayer begins with the words 'Our Father'. This expresses the idea that God cares for us like a father. It also helps people to think of themselves in a close, personal relationship with God. There is no reason why God should not also be thought of as Mother, perhaps reminding people of the loving, self-giving nature of God. A passage from the Bible uses just such an image, where God says:

> As a mother comforts her son,
> so will I myself comfort you.*

Christianity gives us an image of God in the historical person of Jesus. Many people find that other images of God are too difficult,

* *Isaiah 66:13.*

but that they can relate to a real human being. They believe that, in learning about Jesus –his character and what he stood for – they are learning about God.

Let us pray

LORD, we all have our images of you.
Help us to realise that these are *only* images,
which can come nowhere near your true glory.
The New Testament says that 'now we see through a glass darkly'
but, one day, we shall realise what you are really like.
Prepare us, Lord, for that day.

Amen

An easy option?

It is sometimes said that belief in God is wishful thinking. That people turn to religion because they cannot face up to the real world. That it's for weaklings who cling to the idea of God because they need a substitute father.

If you study the history of religions, this opinion does not stand up to the facts. On the contrary, it appears that religion often gives people the will to live their lives for others; and it gives them strength and courage, often to risk dangers and even death for what they believe. It makes demands on people, rather than offering them an easy option.

This is well illustrated in the New Testament story of Pentecost, which was the beginning of the Christian Church. After Jesus' work on earth was finished, his disciples laid low in Jerusalem, unsure what to do next without him. They were waiting for inspiration. When it came, it was with unexpected force. This is how it is described:

> When the Day of Pentecost had come, they were all together in one place. And suddenly a sound came from heaven like the rush of a mighty wind, and it filled all the house where they were sitting. And there appeared to them tongues as of fire, distributed and resting on each one of them. And they were all filled with the Holy Spirit.*

The Spirit of God is described in the symbols of wind and fire. God struck them like a gale, driving them out from their refuge on to the streets of Jerusalem to proclaim their faith in Jesus Christ. He was like a raging inferno, setting each of them on fire with the Christian message. These were the first of many Christians to face persecution for their beliefs.

But even when people's lives are not put at risk by their religion, they still find that God demands much of them. Their work – their time – their money – all that they are and all that they have, should come under the control of their religious beliefs. Perhaps, after all, religion is for the courageous rather than the faint-hearted. Perhaps it

* *Acts 2:1–4.*

demands too much of many of us, who don't want our own cosy way of life to be challenged.

Let us pray

Yours, LORD, is the greatness, the power, the glory, the victory and the majesty; for everything in heaven and on earth is yours. All wealth and honour come from you, for you rule over all. All power and might are in your hand; and you are able to make anyone great and strong. And now we give you thanks, O God, and praise your glorious name.*

Amen

* *Adapted from 1 Chronicles 29:11–13.*

What are they worth?

Do you believe in anything strongly enough, not only to live for it, but also to die for it? The following story comes from the Second World War:

> Franz Jaggerstatter was born in 1907 in the small Austrian village of St Radegund, where he worked as a peasant farmer and caretaker of the Catholic parish church. He married a girl from a nearby village in 1936. In 1938 when Hitler's troops moved into Austria, Jaggerstatter was the only man in the village to vote against the takeover of Austria by the Nazis, and he publicly said that he believed the Nazi movement was an evil thing.
>
> Jaggerstatter was called up for military service in 1943. Although his friends and the parish priest tried to persuade him, he refused to take the oath of loyalty to Hitler on the grounds that it would be wrong for him as a Christian to do so and to fight for Nazism. He was imprisoned first at Linz and then at Berlin and, after a military trial, was beheaded on 9 August 1943, leaving a wife and three daughters – the eldest not quite six years old. In his last letter from prison he wrote, 'I cannot contribute to an unjust war. May God accept my life as a penance for my sins and those of others.'

It was another twenty years before this story became known outside that Austrian village. Perhaps it would not have mattered to Franz Jaggerstatter if it had never become known, for this was something he had to do anyway. Do you think he was right to stand by his beliefs and to speak out against evil – at such a price? If you were his children, growing up without a father, what would you think of his sacrifice?

Let us pray

LORD, such faith and courage reduces us to silence. We pray that we will never be tested to such an extent, but that examples like this will inspire us in our everyday lives to uphold what we know to be good, true and worthwhile.

Amen

Superstition

Some people are afraid of Friday the 13th; of walking under ladders; of breaking a mirror; of crossing on the stairs. . . . These are just some of the things considered to be unlucky. You can take precautions against bad luck by having lucky charms in the shape of horseshoes, black cats, Cornish pixies, St Christophers and so on. A lot of lucky mascots appear in school during examinations!

All of this is *superstition*: the irrational belief in supernatural powers. Sometimes *religion* is classed as superstition, but really there is a world of difference between the two. Superstition is when you believe you are affected by supernatural powers outside yourself, either good or bad, and that you can control these forces by doing the right thing – like crossing your fingers, or throwing salt over your shoulder.

Religious people also believe in supernatural, or spiritual, forces. They believe there is more to life than the solid, material things of our physical world. They live their lives in the belief that they are supported and surrounded by that divine power which called them into being. But religion is not like a lucky charm – it does not miraculously protect them from harm; and belonging to a religion does not automatically guarantee them a place in heaven. They do religious things, like being baptised, or taking Holy Communion on Sundays, *not* because this will bring them good luck, but because this is a way of expressing their beliefs and of worshipping God.

Let us pray

Let us think carefully about our own beliefs, and the actions connected with them. May we not be ruled by irrational fears, but respond both to reason and intuition.

Amen

NATURE

Awe and wonder

The sense of awe and wonder at the splendour of nature was one of the first religious feelings experienced by human beings. That does not mean it is out of place in our modern world. The astronaut, Colonel James Irwin, gives us some of his thoughts when he was on the moon:

> Each night, when we bedded down in the lunar module, I would lie awake for a few minutes and reflect on the beauty of what I had seen, and try to etch in my mind a lasting impression of the majesty of those mountains.
>
> Running through my reflections like the refrain of a hymn were the words from my favourite Biblical passage, from Psalms: 'I will lift up mine eyes unto the hills, from whence cometh my help. My help cometh from the Lord, who hath made heaven and earth.'
>
> I have encountered nothing on Apollo 15, or in this age of space and science, that dilutes my faith in God. While I was on the moon, in fact, I felt a sense of inspiration.

Coming down to earth, we too can be inspired by the wonders of nature, if only we would quieten ourselves to take it in. Here, a twelve-year-old girl describes a special visit while on holiday in the Isle of Wight:

> I had not believed that there could have been such a beautiful and peaceful place. A completely new world to me which, when I think of it, now seems so far away.
>
> It was a whole world of flying wonders, butterflies large, small, dull and colourful. All special in their own way. I was surrounded by tropical plants, fountains and streams. So hard to believe I was only in the Isle of Wight. But what amazed me most was the quietness of the large glasshouse. There wasn't just me in there but a whole group of people, each and every one of them, sharing the same experience.

Let us pray

LORD, help us to see afresh the beauty that surrounds us,
and to take time to ponder it in wonder and in awe;
for 'the heavens are telling the glory of God,
and the earth proclaims your handiwork.'

Amen

Miracles

Do you believe in miracles? I suppose it all depends on how you define 'miracle', on your powers of philosophy, on how sceptical you are by nature, or how gullible, and on your whole attitude and approach to life.

This poet has no problem in believing in the miracle of nature:

Why, who makes much of a miracle?
As to me I know of nothing else but miracles,
Whether I walk the streets of Manhattan,
Or dart my sight over the roofs of houses toward the sky,
Or wade with naked feet along the beach just in the edge of the water,
Or stand under trees in the woods,
Or watch honey-bees around the hive on a summer forenoon,
Or animals feeding in the fields,
Or birds, or the wonderfulness of insects in the air,
Or the wonderfulness of the sundown, or of the stars shining so quiet
and bright,
Or the exquisite delicate thin curve of the new moon in spring;
These with the rest, one and all, are to me miracles,
The whole referring, yet each distinct and in its place.

To me every hour of the light and dark is a miracle,
Every cubic inch of space is a miracle,
Every square yard of the surface of the earth is spread with the same,
Every foot of the interior swarms with the same.

To me the sea is a continual miracle,
The fishes that swim – the rocks – the motion of the waves – ships with
men in them,
What stranger miracles are there?

Let us pray

O GOD, we thank you for this earth, our home;
for the wide sky and the blessed sun,
for the salt sea and the running water,

for the everlasting hills and the never-resting winds,
for trees and the common grass underfoot.
We thank you for our senses,
by which we hear the songs of the birds,
and see the splendour of the summer fields,
and taste of the autumn fruits,
and rejoice in the feel of the snow,
and smell the breath of the spring.
Grant us a heart wide open to all this beauty
and save our souls from being so blind
that we pass through the world unseeing
and unaware of the miracle of nature.

Amen

Thanksgiving

The following reading is from a Psalm of praise, thanking God for the harvest:

> You visit the earth and water it,
> you load it with riches;
> God's rivers brim with water
> to provide their grain.
> This is how you provide it:
> by drenching its furrows, by levelling its ridges,
> by softening it with showers, and blessing its growth.
> You crown the year with your bounty,
> the palm-trees drip with sweet juice;
> the desert pastures overflow,
> the hillsides are wrapped in joy,
> the meadows are clothed with sheep
> and the valleys mantled in corn;
> they shout and sing together for joy!*

We give thanks for the generosity of nature, which provides us with such a variety of good things to eat:

The soft fruits and crisp salads of summer
are followed by crunchy apples and nuts of autumn
and the staple root vegetables and leafy greens of winter.
Exotic fruits and vegetables add to this variety,
coming to us from all round the world:
shiny purple aubergines and red peppers,
avocado pears, and Sharon fruit from Israel,
melons and juicy citron fruits,
green Kiwi fruit from New Zealand,
mangoes from the Caribbean –
all can be found on the supermarket shelf.
Rich colours to catch the eye,
unusual shapes and textures to the touch.

We give thanks for the abundance of nature

* *Psalm 65:9–13.*

and our ability to work in harmony with it.
Bringing food fresh from the other side of the world,
preserving and transporting it in many ways.
Making the grain into bread,
the grape into wine.
Bringing irrigation to arid lands
and nutrients to barren soil.
Reclaiming the marshlands and making deserts bloom.

We give thanks for the imagination
of those who concoct interesting recipes,
producing delicious combinations of tastes and smells.

We give thanks that *we* have no shortage of food,
that we have money to buy it,
and appetites to enjoy it.
And in celebrating the generosity of nature,
we too want to give generously out of our abundance,
to share with those who do not yet enjoy the earth's riches.

Let us pray

Blessed are you, LORD our God, King of the universe,
who gives us the fruits of the earth.

Amen

Conservation

We spray the fields and scatter
    The poison on the ground,
So that no wicked wild flowers
    Upon our farm be found.
We like whatever helps us
    To line our purse with pence;
The twenty-four-hour broiler-house
    And neat electric fence.

This parody of the famous harvest hymn, in John Betjeman's unmistakable style, is saying that our concern for making money often overrides our care for nature; and short-term gains often have devastating, long-term results.

The same point is made in this passage, by a Red Indian leader, Chief Seattle:

> We know that the white man does not understand our ways. One portion of land is the same to him as the next, for he is a stranger who comes in the night and takes from the land whatever he needs. The earth is not his brother but his enemy, and when he has conquered it, he moves on. . . . He treats his mother, the earth, and his brother, the sky, as things to be bought, plundered, sold like sheep or bright beads. His appetite will devour the earth and leave behind only a desert.
>
> I do not know. Our ways are different from your ways. The sight of your cities pains the eyes of the red man. But perhaps it is because the red man is a savage and does not understand.

Let us pray

Is it primitive –
To respect Mother Earth which sustains us; or to lay it waste?
To care for all living things while we have them; or to regret that they have become extinct?
To conserve natural resources; or to leave a legacy of danger and pollution?
Give us, LORD, a vision and a hope –

'Vision to discover a new and caring relationship with the rest of our living world; and hope that the destruction of nature can be stopped before all is wasted and lost.'*

Amen

* *From Prince Philip's speech at the World Wildlife Fund's twenty-fifth anniversary conference in Assisi.*

LIGHT

A symbol

Light is often a part of our celebrations, especially at those festivals which take place in the dark winter season. Candles on a cake; lights on a tree; fireworks lighting up the night sky; strings of coloured light-bulbs turning the most ordinary place into a fairyland – all these add to the happiness and excitement as we celebrate important events.

This poem by an eleven-year-old schoolgirl speaks of some of the good things we associate with light, in contrast to darkness:

DARKNESS to me means:
The empty feeling of losing a friend
Or someone I love.
The despairing feeling of not being able to help,
Just standing
Helplessly.

DARKNESS to me means:
An angry, dull day,
Or when the wind is howling,
The rain pelting down,
Making it wet and sad.

BUT

LIGHT means to me:
Happiness and joy,
Laughing and singing,
A birthday or Christmas wish,
Loving and sharing.

LIGHT means to me:
Warmth on a cold night,
Romance . . . passion
And
Caring.

Let us pray

The LORD bless us and keep us,
The Lord make his face to shine upon us
and be gracious to us,
The Lord lift up the light of his countenance upon us,
and give us his peace.*

Amen

* *Adapted from Numbers 6:24–6.*

The inner light

Do you ever know that something is right, even when there is no proof? Do you ever sense that there is something you have to do, even if your friends think you are mad to do it? There are times when we have an inner conviction like this; an inner certainty of a truth we cannot prove or explain, sometimes that we don't even fully understand.

George Fox, founder of the Society of Friends (or Quakers), spoke of the 'inner light' – the truth that burns in the heart of every person – the divine spark in each one of us. It is often uncomfortable, so we may try to ignore it. We can go against it, and then we feel guilty. But some people have the courage to follow their inner light. It gives them a sense of purpose, even in the most confusing and difficult times.

Sydney Carter wrote a song about George Fox. Here are two verses from it:

There's a light that is shining
In the heart of a man,
There's a light that was shining
When the world began.
There's a light that is shining
In the Turk and the Jew
And a light that is shining, friend,
In me and in you.

There's an ocean of darkness
And I drown in the night
Till I come through the darkness
To the ocean of light.
You can lock me in prison
But the light will be free,
'And I walk in the glory
Of the light,' said he.

Let us pray

Lead me from the unreal to the real;
Lead me from darkness to light;
Lead me from death to immortality.*

Amen

* *From the Upanishads.*

In the darkness

However bad things get, religious people find reassurance in their faith in God. Frank Topping, a Methodist minister and broadcaster, expresses it like this:

And there always is a light
As we plot our way through weeks and years,
Through the storms of our calling,
Through failure and disappointment,
Even in the dark nights of suffering,
Even in the face of death,
We pray, and there is light,
A greater light than we expected,
Guiding us to havens and to rest.

In the Book of Psalms, which is used by both Jews and Christians, God is described as this light which banishes fear and brings us to safety. We shall use this psalm as our prayer.

Let us pray

The LORD is my light and my help;
whom shall I fear?
The Lord is the stronghold of my life;
before whom shall I shrink?

When evil-doers draw near
to devour my flesh,
it is they, my enemies and foes,
who stumble and fall.

Though an army encamp against me
my heart would not fear.
Though war break out against me
even then would I trust.

I am sure I shall see the Lord's goodness
in the land of the living.
Hope in him, hold firm and take heart.
Hope in the Lord!*

Amen

* *Psalm 26:1–3, 13–14.*

The light of my life

There are certain people who are lights in our lives. When we are children, our parents or guardians are usually our lights – leading us forward and showing us the way to go. As we grow up, we may find other people as well, who help to guide us in our decisions. Or they may enlighten our understanding about important things, or spark off ideas in us. When we feel gloomy, we may have special friends who are like rays of hope. They have the ability to look on the bright side of life and to cheer us up.

Grandparents often speak of the joy that their grandchildren bring them – brightening up the last part of their lives, after their own children have left home. It works the other way too. In this account, Kathryn, who is eleven, describes the warmth of her grandmother's personality:

> The people who have put light in my life are all the people I love and like; but one person who brings light into everybody's life is my Grandma.
>
> My Grandma is affectionate, lovable and understanding. She listens to all my problems and tries to help. I also find that she is ready to keep any secret, even if she does not agree.
>
> The most important thing about my Grandma is that, even if I'm feeling grumpy, bored, fed up or sad, and no one can make me smile – one smile from my Grandma and it's impossible to keep a down face any longer, and she soon has me laughing and cheerful.

Apart from all the people we know personally, who are lights in our lives, there are the great people who are recognised as lights of the world. We can think of famous people in our own day who have devoted their lives to helping others. We can think of famous musicians, artists and writers of the past, whose work still brings pleasure to countless people.

The great religious leaders are seen as lights of the world, bringing new insights and inspiration. They have acted like beacons on a hill: warning us of disaster if we continue to lead selfish lives; and spreading the message that there is hope for the world in the ways of justice and of peace.

Let us pray

Thank you, LORD, for all who have brought light into our lives:
Those who are special to us personally,
And those who have been an inspiration to the whole of humanity.
Help each of us, in our own way, to shine in the world,
And to bring happiness to those around us.

Amen